The memoirs of Milton Shulman, *Marilyn, Hitler and Me*, were only recently published and were his eleventh book. His first, *Defeat in the West*, recognized as a classic account of the defeat of the German Army in World War Two, was published in 1947 and is still in print. He lives in central London. His wife is the journalist, Drusilla Beyfus, and they have three children, Alexandra, Nicola and Jason.

# VOLTAIRE, GOLDBERG
## & OTHERS

A Compendium of the Witty, the
Profound and the Absurd

Collected by

# MILTON SHULMAN

Quartet Books

First published by Quartet Books in 1999
A member of the Namara Group
27 Goodge Street
London W1P 2LD

This edition published by Quartet Books in 2000

A catalogue record for this book is available from the
British Library

ISBN 0 7043 8149 4

Printed and bound in Great Britain by Cox & Wyman,
Reading, Berks

# Contents

## List of illustrations by Vicky

To my grandchildren, Sybilla (7), John (5), Sam (4) and Thomas (2), who I hope one day will share the fun and exhilaration these pages gave their grandfather.

# Introduction

Everyone has favourite anecdotes, cherished moments, banal truisms, profound observations, unforgettable lyrics, best jokes, scraps from newspapers that they write down or keep in their heads for conversation and information. Laced with snatches from the classics – Ovid, Seneca, Tennyson, Macaulay, Molière *et al.* – they are often assembled in commonplace books which display the fancies of the erudite or well-read mind. *Voltaire, Goldberg and Others* has a more contemporary goal. With an occasional obeisance to the classics, it tries to preserve in book form the many perceptive, amusing, clever, satirical, descriptive, hilarious, weighty, wise and erudite treasures that often appear in newspapers and periodicals or are heard on television and radio. It is my hope that by being preserved in a book, some of them may escape oblivion. 'Compendium' seems to be the most pertinent collective noun to describe this collection.

I have perused, skipped through or glanced at six or seven newspapers – English but some American – every day for almost fifty years. At first as a learning aid, then as information and inspiration for my work as a journalist and finally for enjoyment and exasperation.

Based upon my work in British and Canadian Intelligence and my interrogations of senior German commanders like von Rundstedt, I wrote the first account of the war from a German military standpoint. It was called *Defeat in the West* and was published in 1947. It was a considerable success and it is still in print and selling over fifty years later. While waiting for it to be published, I decided I would try my hand at being a journalist – I had been a lawyer in Toronto – and through various strokes of luck managed to land myself on the foreign desk of Reuters News Agency. A few months later, I joined the London *Evening Standard*.

It was when I was preparing myself for this new career that I realized that my intimate knowledge of the English was totally inadequate for a career commenting on the social and political issues that interested newspaper readers. I had been in the Canadian army for over five years and knew little about what was going on on the domestic scene in Britain. I had to know more about the significant political and cultural figures, the customs, tastes and foibles of the average reader; needed knowledge about its arcane games, like cricket, and the vernacular, jargon and slang of the media and the people. I decided that the best way of educating myself about this new and exciting environment was to read newspapers and magazines and to listen to the radio. Television was in its infancy at that time.

Trawling through these acres of newsprint I was constantly being startled or fascinated by some news story or gracious piece of writing that I wanted to remember or refer to. I would write them down in a simple, lined notebook under headings like Theatre, Politics, War, Women. I would supplement them with remembered phrases, jokes and *pensées* from my reading of biographies, histories and novels.

The selections in *Voltaire, Goldberg and Others* are in no way comprehensive of the many decades of my casual reading. There was one period in the 1960s, when I was busy with two jobs as a theatre critic and television executive for Granada and Rediffusion, in which hardly a single entry was made. It was only when my first notebook was full and a second one started that I began in the early 1990s to harbour thoughts of a book. I began to realize that most of these literary and anecdotal gems would eventually be shredded – as my cuttings have been – or stuffed away in some newspaper museum with difficult access. That would be a pity. I decided to preserve those items that intrigued me.

Journalists are a self-deprecating lot. They rejoice in calling themselves hacks and scribblers. Yet libraries overflow with the collected journalists' efforts. Some of the most respected names in English literature have had their topical articles and reflections – dashed off to meet some crucial deadline – preserved for posterity in their books. Swift, Hazlitt, Belloc, Chesterton, Beerbohm, Mencken, Cyril Connolly, Ken Tynan, Orwell – to skim off the top a few names from this heap of great writers who owe their fame to their toiling in the vineyards of journalism. Contemporary columnists like Bernard Levin, Peregrine Worsthorne, Paul Johnson, Matthew Parris, William Rees-Mogg, Simon Jenkins, Jill Tweedie, Frank Johnson, Howard Jacobson, Alan Coren, Victor Lewis-Smith, Miles Kington have already had their pieces enshrined between hard covers. Someday many of them will become required reading for matriculation or undergraduate courses and attain the status of Orwell or Belloc. There are, of course, hundreds of other journalists, who have not had the luck of acquiring a column or a regular slot in a newspaper, whose incidental articles contain a paragraph or anecdote that made me go back and read it again. Usually before transcribing it into my notebook I would test it on my wife or a colleague. If they smiled, chuckled or nodded approval, in it would go. Sometimes I disregarded the test and relied entirely on my own judgement. But not often.

Occasionally I would come across a story that I remembered hearing long ago and had to decide whether it should go into the notebook even though it would be familiar, almost a cliché, to many people. This dilemma was acute when it came to repeating the jokes or familiar witticisms of Oscar Wilde or Noël Coward. I took solace in the words of the writer and humorist A P Herbert: 'Don't stop me if you've heard this one before,' he wrote. 'There is no reason why a joke should not be appreciated more than once. Imagine how little good music there would be if, for example, a conductor refused to play Beethoven's Fifth Symphony on the grounds that his audience might have heard it before.'

Every generation has to hear a witticism, a repartee or a joke for the first time. A five-year-old will fall about when he is asked, 'Why did the chicken cross the road?' and hears the punchline, 'To get to the other side.' I would guess that ninety-nine per cent of the world's population has not heard every joke that they might hear. The reason some of the most popular and witty observations have not been included is not because I fear readers will have heard them before – Groucho Marx 'I wouldn't join a club that would have me as a member' – but because they have been repeated *ad nauseam* in dozens of recent books of quotations. However, it would be misleading about my judgement, if I did not record some of the classic remarks made by raconteurs and wits – old as they may be – that gave me pleasure and delight. In my chapter 'You've Heard It Before', I list some of the familiar sayings that many cultivated or well-read people have heard before. They are, of course, only a sample of the output of these famous names.

But in the last analysis, I must take the responsibility or the blame for what I have selected for my compendium. Readers who share my sense of humour, love the incongruous, are amused by the eccentric, are in awe of the profound, dazzled by the quick-witted, diverted by the accidental, enchanted by gracious writing, should, I hope, find a great deal of entertainment in these pages.

# A BAG OF TRICKS
*(Actors and Acting)*

Sir Ralph Richardson had been cast as Kitchener in the film
*Khartoum*. The star of the film as General Gordon was
Charlton Heston, who had appeared as Moses and Ben-Hur
on the screen. At a cocktail party in London given for Heston,
Richardson was introduced to him as the star of the
forthcoming picture. 'Ah yes,' said Richardson, studying him
carefully. 'I remember you now. I've often seen you in trailers.'

\* \* \*

When a magazine telegraphed Cary Grant with the question:
'How old Cary Grant?' Grant is supposed to have replied, 'Old
Cary Grant fine, how you?'
The Times, 18.1.84, page 8

\* \* \*

An actor is an interpreter of other men's words, often a soul
which wishes to reveal itself to the world but dare not, a
craftsman, a bag of tricks, a vanity bag, a cool observer of mankind, a child, and at best a kind of unfrocked priest who, for an
hour or two, can call on heaven and hell to mesmerize a group
of innocents.
Alec Guinness, *Blessings in Disguise* (Hamish Hamilton, 1985)

\* \* \*

Alec Guinness is very difficult to interview and has humanely solved this problem by not giving interviews, thus preserving at a blow the privacy of the artist and the sanity of the press. His attitude is that of the ghost in *Hamlet*: 'Speak!' 'It is offended.' 'Stay, speak, speak, I charge thee speak!' Exit ghost, who won't talk to just any Tom, Dick or Horatio.

Nancy Banks-Smith, *Guardian*, 7.10.85

\* \* \*

Kenneth More, on tour with a repertory company, had just completed arrangements for bed and board at a provincial boarding house. 'Do you have a good memory for faces, Mr More?' asked the landlady, leading him to his room. 'Yes, yes,' said the puzzled actor, 'I think so.' 'That's good,' came the reply, 'because there's no mirror in the bathroom.'

Told by Brian Forbes at Kenneth More's memorial service, 20 September 1982

\* \* \*

Acting is merely the art of keeping a large group of people from coughing.

Ralph Richardson, quoted in *Ralph Richardson* by Larry O'Connor, page 130

\* \* \*

Orson Welles, who had played Falstaff a number of times, went backstage to congratulate Sir Ralph Richardson after his Falstaff at the Old Vic in 1945. 'Thought I'd done all right as Falstaff,' said Welles, 'but the thing I must say, Ralph, I never matched you at the end. I could never do that because I haven't got your blue eyes.' Welles, his own eyes resting on Ralph's face, paused a moment. 'By God,' he then said very quietly, 'you haven't *got* blue eyes.'

Larry O'Connor, ibid., page 124

When Orson Welles found himself in a situation where he was expected to say something complimentary to a person whose performance he had loathed, he would grasp the actor's hand and warmly say, 'Words fail me!'

Told by Orson Welles to Milton Shulman

\* \* \*

Paul Newman the actor was standing at a urinal when a stranger standing next to him asked for his autograph. 'That was the terminal insult,' Newman recalls. 'That's when I stopped giving autographs.'

BBC TV interview on *Film 82*

\* \* \*

David Frost, as master of ceremonies at one of the annual awards for media personalities, claims that a special award was on its way to the actress, Pia Zadora, whose performance in an off-Broadway revival of *The Diary of Anne Frank* was so bad that when the Gestapo arrived the entire audience shouted: 'She's in the attic.'

Peterborough, *Daily Telegraph*, 18.4.84

\* \* \*

Ingrid Bergman on film conquered all our young hearts by holding out a certain kind of sexual promise where lust and reason need not cancel out each other.

Clancy Sigal, obituary for Ingrid Bergman, *Guardian*, 31.8.82

\* \* \*

Her name, cut clear upon this marble cross,
Shines as it shone when she was still on earth;
While tenderly the mild, agreeable moss
Obscures the figures of her date of birth.

Dorothy Parker on an actress's tombstone

Ingrid Bergman had a superabundance of all the virtues of the Swedes – innocence, romanticism and emotional recklessness – and all their faults – innocence, romanticism and emotional recklessness.

Sam White commenting in the *Evening Standard* on her elopement with director Roberto Rossellini

★ ★ ★.

Robert Morley met an old friend, fellow actor Llewellyn Rees, whom he hadn't seen for some time. 'It's nice meeting old friends,' said Rees warmly. 'A lot of people think I'm dead.' 'Not if you look closely,' said Morley.

*Faber Book of Anecdotes*, 1985

★ ★ ★

It was said of Errol Flynn that you knew where you stood with him. He always let you down.

Godfrey Barker, *Daily Telegraph*, 19.2.87

★ ★ ★

John Gilbert, the great screen lover of silent films, could learn his lines for stage parts, but always forgot the proper names. He was called upon at short notice to play the part of the heroine's father in a Chicago production. He learned the lines in record time but was still struggling to remember the name of the character he was playing, Numitorius, when the play opened. A colleague suggested the Book of Numbers as a mnemonic. Gilbert strode on stage with renewed confidence on the first night and delivered his opening line: 'Hold, 'tis I, her father – Deuteronomy.'

Philip Howard, *The Times*, 20.4.87

★ ★ ★

She looks like the sort of woman who could eat an apple through a tennis racket.

Film director about actress with prominent teeth

★ ★ ★

Great actors have a latent power to disturb.

Antony Quayle, quoted by Paul Ferris in his biography of Richard Burton

★ ★ ★

Oscar Levant, American writer and wit, was in the dressing room of an actress who had just finished a first night performance. Her friends were showering her with congratulations but Oscar sat silently in a corner of the dressing room. He was approached by the star's husband.

'And what did you think of her, Oscar?' asked the husband.

'I think she stinks,' said Levant.

'And who are you to say she stinks?' replied the outraged husband.

'And who do the hell you have to be to say she stinks?' asked Levant.

Told to Milton Shulman

★ ★ ★

As a young actor in the 1930s, Robert Morley became a member of the touring company lead by Frank Benson, the legendary Shakespearean actor. Benson was now approaching the end of a long career and his diction wasn't all it might have been, except when he was playing Caliban, the earthly monster in *The Tempest*. In that role, Morley recalled, Benson's voice miraculously came out marvellously clear. 'We all went into the wings to see what had caused the improvement,' Morley recalls. 'There was Benson, hanging upside down in a tree as Caliban, and for the first and only time on the whole tour his false teeth fitted him properly.'

Profile of his father by Sheridan Morley, *The Times*, 25.5.78

'I suppose, dear,' called the actress Gladys Cooper to her daughter Joan, when she heard of her engagement to Robert Morley in 1940, 'if you love him he can't be altogether disastrous.'

Ibid.

* * *

Denying that cocaine was habit-forming, Tallulah Bankhead said, 'I've been taking it for seventeen years and I ought to know.'

Quoted in *Louise Brooks* by Barry Paris

* * *

Robert Morley had made an appearance as the victim in the TV show *This is your Life* which is a nostalgia exercise in which friends and admirers of the central figure voice their admiration for him. Meeting him the next morning, the actor Rex Harrison congratulated him on the show. 'So brave of you,' he said. 'I would never do one of those, not with all my ex-wives. But then of course, Robert, it's all been so different for you: one wife, one family, one house and, if I may say so, one performance.'

Sheridan Morley, op. cit.

* * *

I remember my young brother once saying, 'I'd like to marry Elizabeth Taylor,' and my father said, 'Don't worry, your turn will come.'

Spike Milligan, *Guardian*, 27.2.88

* * *

There was a celebrated *Tempest* performed in the open air at an Oxford college. As described to me by friends who saw it (interestingly, they don't quite agree on the details), when the spirit Ariel made his departure from the play he ran across the stage which backed on to the college lake, and when he got to the edge of the lake he just kept running, along the surface of the water, that is to say along the boards cunningly placed just below the surface – plish, plash, plish, plash, into the enfolding dark, and, as he became lost to view, from the further shore a firework rocket went *whoosh* into the sky and the rocket burst into sparks, and the sparks went out, and Ariel had gone.

The written-down version of this is: 'Exit Ariel.' Shakespeare would have loved it, and I think would have felt complimented that the text inspired an event which changes the experience of returning to the text.

Tom Stoppard, *Weekend Telegraph*, 23.4.88

\* \* \*

Demonstrating the professionalism of Marlene Dietrich, her impresario, Robert Pattison, told me of a final dress rehearsal of her one-woman show at the Palladium when Marlene insisted the orchestra all turned up in the evening dress they would wear at the first night. During her performance, there was a short blackout to enable her to turn up in a startling white light. She insisted on seeing the effect from the stalls in which even the exit signs were blacked out. On getting back on stage she asked for a brush and a bucket of black paint. She then approached the first violinist and between the top of his socks and his trouser leg, she painted in black the expanse of white skin which she claimed had spoiled the total blackout effect.

Told to Milton Shulman by Robert Pattison, Garrick, April 1988

\* \* \*

# Actors' nightmares

The play seems familiar but everyone is speaking French.

The one I always love is of not being able to find the stage: going down corridors and through doors and finally ending up in the lobby.

My worst nightmare is that the audience is entirely composed of critics, other actors and directors.

Without fail, before playing an important role, I dream I go on in completely the wrong costume and I don't know the play at all... It happened this season with *Romeo and Juliet*: everyone else was in dinner jackets and cocktail dresses and I was in a Roman soldier's uniform.

I'm fine until about halfway through the play and then they start to change the ending and I'm fighting for my life to keep up, find my place and keep the audience fooled. What is horrible is the dream is always permanently in the middle and it never ends...

Programme notes for an RSC production at the Barbican of *A Midsummer Night's Dream*, 13.8.87

★ ★ ★

# Remarks about plays by audiences

Two men leaving the Old Vic after the opening of the Peter O'Toole *Macbeth*: 'All I hope now is the dog hasn't been sick in the car.'

At Stratford-upon-Avon after the curtain fell on the heap of corpses at the end of a long and not wonderful *Antony and Cleopatra*, a woman remarked: 'The very same thing happened to Maureen.'

Sheridan Morley, *The Times*, 14.4.88

★ ★ ★

Max Adrian, the actor, told of a production he was in, in London in May 1945, just when the war officially ended, and the cast received a telegram from their director, John Gielgud, who was in New York: 'All those entering upstage right enter down left and vice versa. Wonderful news. Love. John.'

Patrick Garland reviewing *Gielgud* by Robert Tanich, *Spectator*, 7.5.88

★ ★ ★

When Marie Lloyd, the Edwardian music-hall comedienne, sang 'She sits among the cabbages and peas,' her theatre manager insisted she drop the line and sing something cleaner. She came back and sang the next night, 'She sits among the cabbages and leeks.'

Anon

★ ★ ★

In his one man show, Peter Ustinov told how Alec Guinness, 'a mysterious, demure, and secretive man', was obsessed by a desire to play Adolf Hitler and was upset to learn Dustin Hoffman was likely to get the part. Guinness, to prove his ability to play Hitler, dressed himself in a Nazi uniform, hired a cameraman and in Little Venice in London paraded up and down as Hitler for his private screen-test. Passers-by took no notice of this peculiar demonstration except for a constable who ambled up to him and said, 'Excuse me, sir, is that your car on a double yellow line?' Guinness said it was. After a long pause the constable said, 'Well, I'd give you a ticket, sir, but I don't want to find myself in a concentration camp.'

Peter Ustinov at the Haymarket, 23.3.90

\* \* \*

Laurence Olivier came to my dressing room and said it was very awkward for him to go to the theatre nowadays because people kept recognizing him, especially in the Olivier Theatre where everyone would be nudging and pointing. I said, 'Why don't you wear a big hat and dark glasses?' He said yes, he'd tried that, 'but nobody recognized me'.

Paul Eddington's memoirs, So Far, So Good (Hodder & Stoughton, 1995)

\* \* \*

Tarquin Olivier, eldest son of Laurence Olivier, was introduced to a Texan businessman. 'Tarquin Olivier,' said the Texan. 'Now there's a name that smacks of overkill.'

Told by Tarquin Olivier to Milton Shulman

\* \* \*

What when drunk one sees in other women, one sees in Garbo sober.

Kenneth Tynan

\* \* \*

A friend is alleged to have told Edmund Kean on his deathbed that he would soon be better. Kean said: 'Why pretend? I know very well that I'm a dying man.' Embarrassed by what he could not deny, the friend murmured something about how difficult that must be for the ailing actor. 'No, No,' Kean said. 'Dying isn't difficult; comedy is difficult.'

Frederick Raphael, review of Humour in Society, Sunday Times, 19.6.88

**Sir Laurence Olivier**

I knew Doris Day before she became a virgin.

Oscar Levant

\* \* \*

Winning a battle for a London taxi, the actress Coral Browne settled into her seat while her frustrated rival continued to protest that he had hailed the cab first. The driver was on Coral's side. 'I think,' he said, 'the lady hailed me first.' 'Which lady?' asked the man. 'This fuckin' lady,' announced Coral as they drove off.

*Spectator*, 8.6.91, page 19

\* \* \*

When the film *An Englishman Abroad* was shown in America the reaction was enthusiastic. Coral Browne attended a Hollywood party at which an indifferent writer came up to congratulate her. 'I loved your performance,' he cooed, 'and I thought Alan was superb...and John's direction was just exquisite...the only thing that worried me just a little, just a little, was the quality of the writing.' 'The quality of the writing?' she exploded. 'You couldn't write "fuck" in the dust on a Venetian blind!'

*Spectator*, 8.6.91

\* \* \*

When Coral Browne attended the first night of a Peter Brook production, the opening scene revealed a huge phallus about fifteen feet high. 'No one we know,' said Coral to her companion at this amazing sight.

*Spectator*, 8.6.98

# When the Pope Starts
# Looking Young
*(Age)*

Pat Kirwan, a Fleet Street journalist, went to Devon to do a profile of Hilaire Belloc for his paper. He found the great essayist and wit in a chair moodily gazing into a coal fire. 'They used to tell me,' he muttered, 'that one of the consolations of old age . was recalling the triumphs and glories of one's youth... but I can't remember a damn thing.'

\* \* \*

The pleasures of youth are not real pleasures and the compensations of old age are not real compensations.
Osbert Lancaster, interviewed in *The Times*, 11.10.82

\* \* \*

When it was once suggested by some eager young Conservative smearmonger that the Tories might discredit Lord Palmerston by producing evidence of a furtive love affair, Disraeli made the famous reply: 'Palmerston is now seventy. If he could produce evidence of his potency in his electoral address, he'd sweep the country.'
Alexander Chancellor, *Spectator*, 11.6.83, page 4

\* \* \*

The eighty-four-year-old Argentine author, Jorge Luis Borges, was asked why he did not commit suicide on 25 August 1983, as he wrote he would in a 1977 story. 'Laziness and cowardice

prevent me,' he said. 'Besides I am constantly falling in love.'
*Time*, 5.9.83

★ ★ ★

Malcolm Muggeridge always liked a particular cartoon submitted to him when he was editor of *Punch*. It had a very elderly man in bed with a rather young and luscious female, and he was saying to her: 'Pass me my teeth and I'll bite you.'
*Sunday Telegraph*, 4.9.83

★ ★ ★

At the age of seventy-four, Victor Borge the comedian was asked how it felt to be getting older. 'Marvellous,' said Borge. 'It is so much better than the alternative.'
*The Times*, 2.1.84, page 8

★ ★ ★

There are three stages in life: youth, middle-age and you're looking very well.
Anon

★ ★ ★

Whenever a man's friends begin to compliment him about looking young, he may be sure that they think he is growing old.
Anon

★ ★ ★

To me old age is always fifteen years older than I am.
Bernard Levin

★ ★ ★

The older I grow, the more I distrust the familiar doctrine that age brings wisdom.

Anon

*  *  *

I knew I was getting old when the Pope started looking young.

Milton Shulman

*  *  *

> I've grown accustomed to my dentures,
> To my deafness I'm resigned,
> I can cope with my bifocals –
> But how I miss my mind!

Anon., quoted in letter to *The Times*, 6.11.92

*  *  *

Three Frenchmen were discussing the disadvantages of growing old.

'I was a great gourmet,' said the seventy-year-old, 'and loved rich and delicious foods. Now my doctor has put me on a strict diet: no spices, no wine, none of my favourite dishes. It is most depressing.'

'I loved classical music,' said the eighty-year-old, 'but now I'm getting deaf and I can no longer enjoy Beethoven, Mozart, Wagner. It is a great deprivation.'

'Last night I was in bed with my mistress,' said the eighty-five-year-old. 'I said, "Louise, let us make love." "But Pierre," she said, "we made love only fifteen minutes ago." You see, I'm losing my memory.'

Anon

*  *  *

If I had known I was going to live to eighty, I would have taken better care of myself.
George Burns

\* \* \*

Asked his age when a witness at the income-tax trial of Ken Dodd, the comedian, Eric Sykes, a friend, answered, 'I am past my sell-by date.'
Quotes, *Independent*, 15.7.89

\* \* \*

On Alfred Tennyson the Poet Laureate's sixty-second birthday, Emily Tennyson expressed her sweet solicitude for him with the words: 'I think Alfred had a happy birthday though we do not mention it to him.'
*Oxford Book of Ages*, *Sunday Times*, 16.6.85

\* \* \*

No eyes left, no ears, no teeth, no legs, no wind. And how astonishingly well one does without them.
French poet Paul Claudel in his *Journals*

\* \* \*

To be young, really young, takes a very long time.
Picasso, 8.5.88

\* \* \*

Growing old is like being increasingly penalized for a crime you haven't committed.
Antony Powell, *Temporary Kings*

\* \* \*

Now that I am sixty, I see why the idea of elder wisdom has passed from currency.

John Updike, *New Yorker*, quoted in a review, *Independent*, 8.11.92

\* \* \*

23 December 1943 – Chips Channon writes in his diary: 'A Proustian incident. In a Bond Street jewellers, I saw an extraordinary marionette of a woman with a really frightening appearance. I recognized Gladys Marlborough, once the world's most beautiful woman, the toast of Paris, the love of Proust, the *belle amie* of Anatole France. I went up to her, and smiled, and put out my hand which she took shrinkingly and then, breaking into French (as she always did), she said, "Est-ce que je vous connais, Monsieur?" "Yes," I said, "I am Chips." She looked at me, stared vacantly with those famous turquoise eyes that drove men insane with desire, and muttered: "Je n'ai jamais entendu ce nom-là" She flung down a ruby clip she was examining, and bolted from the shop. I remembered how we had been allies for twenty years or more; how she used to telephone me every morning; how we used to lunch with Proust; and the story that D'Annunzio fainted when he saw her, such was her beauty.'

*Independent*, 23.12.93

\* \* \*

Old age is not for sissies.

Lawrence Earl (Canadian journalist)

\* \* \*

The youth versus age factor is a particular characteristic of the drug problem. One of the more famous sayings in the cannabis coteries is: Don't trust anyone over thirty.

Michael Schofield, *The Strange Case of Pot*

\* \* \*

Sir Robin Day said that old age was like waiting in the departure lounge of life. To which I replied, 'Fortunately we are in England and the train is bound to be late.'
Milton Shulman

# Pictures Can't Hurt You

*(Art and Artists)*

In Harriet Walk, in Lowndes Square, where I kept a mews house, was the most beautiful Regency arch which used to tower above my little house; and I was painting this arch one day in my upstairs room, and I went downstairs to my little dining room and the arch of course looked quite different from down below, so I took my painting down and I painted it from down there and then I didn't know whether to paint it from upstairs or down, and so, when I went to the club that day I met (William) Nicholson the painter. 'I've got a problem: I'm painting it from upstairs and I ran down and painted it from downstairs and I wasn't quite sure...another bit from upstairs...a bit from below...is this all right? Shouldn't I make a decision?' 'Perfectly all right,' he said, 'perfectly all right, Ralph, but why run?'

Sir Ralph Richardson interviewed by Larry O'Connor on the BBC, 1969

★ ★ ★

Everything is beautiful, the whole secret lies in knowing how to interpret it.

Pisarro, quoted by Gillian Tindall, *Sunday Times*, 15.9.82

★ ★ ★

In England people take for granted that if you are an artist who is known for drawing circles then they only give you the job when a circle project comes up. The idea that perhaps you might be able to do a square is beyond their recognition.

Allen Jones (painter), *Guardian*, 21.7.82, page 9

★ ★ ★

I have a friend who sings so badly, deaf people refuse to watch his lips move.
Comic on the BBC, 26.9.82

\* \* \*

Is not a patron, my lord, one who looks with unconcern on a man struggling for life in the water and when he has reached ground encumbers him with help?
Samuel Johnson, quoted by Christopher Ricks, *Sunday Times*, 29.7.84, page 40

\* \* \*

Picasso was constantly upsetting the verb to see.
Matta, on Picasso, BBC TV, July 1982

\* \* \*

Architects hate pictures because they ruin the walls.
Ibid.

\* \* \*

Picasso would spit in people's eye but people would frame the spit and sell it.
Ibid.

\* \* \*

Marble and flesh look so different that nude statues need never bring a blush to anyone's cheek.
F T Palgrave (art historian)

\* \* \*

The worst painting can't hurt you; but a bad driver can kill you, a bad judge can send you to the chair, and a bad politician can ruin an entire country. That is why even a bad painting is sacred.
Man Ray

★ ★ ★

Most things in life are moments of pleasure and a lifetime of embarrassment; photography is a moment of embarrassment and a lifetime of pleasure.
Tony Benn in a TV interview, quoted in *Independent*, 21.10.89, page 18

★ ★ ★

In tomorrow's interview I must see if I can sneak in the story about two rival painters in Ancient Greece who presented their respective pictures for judgement to a group of art experts. To protect the paintings from the sun they were covered with cloths. The first picture was unveiled to reveal a marvellously painted bowl of cherries, and to everybody's delight a flock of birds swooped down to peck at the lifelike fruit. That seemed to settle the matter but when the judges made to remove the cloth from the second picture they found to their embarrassment that the cloth itself was a painted one. The townsfolk laughed and awarded the prize to the second painter on the grounds that, whereas his rival had merely fooled the birds, the second had fooled the experts – clearly a time-honoured practice.
Eric Hebborn, (painter of fakes), *Weekend Guardian*, 16.11.91

★ ★ ★

Art is what you can get away with.
Marshall McLuan

★ ★ ★

When a scholar was asked if he had read Arianna Stassinopoulos Huffington's biography of Picasso, *Creator and Destroyer*, he replied, 'I gave up halfway through the author's name.'

Philip French, *Observer*, 5.1.97

# Fishes, Feathers and Fur
*(Animals)*

It is true that enthusiasm is a dangerous characteristic. Lord Melbourne thought it was most undesirable in a cabinet minister. Ronald Knox, in his best book, showed it was often reprehensible in a clergyman. It is unsuitable to many animals. Nobody wants an enthusiastic cat. But an unenthusiastic dog is no good at all.

Paul Johnson, *Daily Telegraph*, 31.8.82

\* \* \*

I loathe people who keep dogs. They are cowards who haven't got the guts to bite people themselves.

August Strindberg, quoted in Nanette Newman's *Dog Lover's Coffee-Table Book*

\* \* \*

'LOST: Brown-and-black dog, blind in left eye, half of right ear missing, no tail and a limp. Answers to the name of Lucky.

Newspaper advertisement quoted by D. Williams, *Spectator*, 9.10.82, page 30

\* \* \*

When George Melly, jazz singer and critic, was taken as a young child to Liverpool zoo, he was seized by an elephant which lifted him high above its head before putting him down gently and eating his aunt's glove. When the aunt complained to the elephant's keeper, he replied: 'I could look for your glove, like, over the next day or two, but you wouldn't want to wear it, would you? Not after where it's been.'

Auberon Waugh reviewing George Melly's *Scouse-Mouse or I Never Got Over It* (Weidenfeld and Nicolson), *Daily Mail*, 29.4.84, page 7

★ ★ ★

The Giant Panda of Peking
Eats only bits of knotted string.
When offered a more balanced diet,
It will not even try it.
The penalty of anorexia
Is it gets steadily unsexier.
When tempted with a nubile mate,
It strangely fails to procreate.
Take warning from the panda's fate
And always eat what's on your plate.

John Craven went to Wolong for *Newsround* ('China: Panda in Peril', BBC1). The panda's problem is a strangely self-induced starvation. They are not only dying in large numbers, they are not being born. 'Pandas aren't very good at breeding and there's been no patter of tiny paws here at the centre,' said Craven. As pandas spend fourteen hours a day eating and the rest sleeping, it is not surprising the birthrate is low. There is something about the panda which does not give you a lot of hope. Under those entertaining baggy white fur bloomers, or in the general vicinity thereof, there beats the suicidal and depressive heart of the true comedian.

Nancy Banks-Smith, *Guardian*, 30.4.86

★ ★ ★

Sir – Two years ago, in a letter which you published on 3 April 1989, I reported to you that the note of the buzz of the bumble bee (*Bombus terrestris*) on 27 March that year was C sharp below middle C.

Today I had the opportunity to listen to the note struck by the same kind of bumble bee and its pitch was a semitone higher, the D below middle C. A year ago I noted it to be the same on 3 April, while the note of a slightly smaller bumble bee was three semitones higher, i.e., F.

G B R Walkley

Letter to *The Times*, 12.4.91

★ ★ ★

The absence of wings is a design fault in the modern pig, though about the only one. If ever dogs had to stand aside as man's best friend, the family *suidae* could take over. The pig's real problem is that man, being a real swine, has not recognized his porcine benefactor for the splendid thing it is. Piggism – irrational prejudice against the creature – is rife.

Does George Orwell want a greedy animal as his ultimate farmyard bully? Does Graham Greene need a silly domestic creature to fall from a balcony? Do militants want to abuse the police; or women, men? The friendless pig will do. If pigs could sue...

Pigs in the natural state are friendly and intelligent creatures, all-consuming and all-consumable – and clean. Pigs and hens are to an English farmyard as bacon and eggs are to an English breakfast. But no pig ever got fat on man's gratitude for services rendered, only on the consumer appetite for lean and succulent pork with plenty of crackling. How many votes are there in cruelty to pigs?

*The Times*, Leader column

★ ★ ★

Sir –

> So, adders now are sacrosanct,
> To them we must be kind.
> Two thousand pounds for killing one
> Is what 'they' have in mind.

An unknown factor still remains
That ought to be defined:
Should adders go on killing us,
Would they in turn be fined?

June Blane, Lewes, E Sussex

Letter to *The Times*, January 1991

# Trouble with Commas

*(Books and Authors)*

We read Anatole France to find out what Anatole France has been reading.

*The Times*, 1.8.85, page 11

\* \* \*

When André Gide was asked the name of the best French poet, he replied: 'Victor Hugo, alas!'

\* \* \*

Israel Zangwill in his preface to one of his novels wrote: 'I am sorry this book is not some other kind of book, but the next one shall be.'

\* \* \*

Philip Hope-Wallace, the journalist, was sent by the British Council to provide some culture for British troops waiting for repatriation after the Second World War. In Cairo two thousand troops were marched in to hear his lecture. He was introduced by a regimental sergeant major who began: 'Mr Hope-Wallace has come from London to give you an interesting talk. His subject is Keats. You are jolly lucky to hear him. I bet none of you bastards knows what a Keat is.'

\* \* \*

Let us reflect whether there be any living writer whose silence we would consider to be a literary disaster.
Cyril Connolly, *The Unquiet Grave* (1944)

★ ★ ★

A good novel tells us the truth about its hero; but a bad novel tells us the truth about its author.
G K Chesterton

★ ★ ★

A well-written *Life* is almost as rare as a well-spent one.
Thomas Carlyle

★ ★ ★

Reviewing Norman Mailer's novel *Ancient Evenings*, Anthony Burgess was fascinated by Mailer's obsession in this book with the concept of the anal passage as a source of magic and power. 'On the only occasion on which I met Mailer,' wrote Burgess, 'he said: "Burgess, your last book was shit." I can see now that he was paying me a compliment.'
Anthony Burgess, *Observer*, 5.6.83

★ ★ ★

Of Karl Marx, historian A J P Taylor wrote: 'Perhaps no other man has owed his reputation to books which nobody reads or has ever heard of.'
Michael Foot, reviewing *An Old Man's Diary*, *Sunday Times*, 22.4.84

★ ★ ★

Asked on one occasion about how he had come to take up writing, Ferenc Molnar the Hungarian playwright said: 'It's the same old story as with many members of a similar profession of entertainer – prostitutes. First I did it out of curiosity, I went on with it for pleasure, and have finally stayed on in it for the money.'

Programme note for Tom Stoppard's play, *Rough Crossing*, National Theatre, November 1984

\* \* \*

Father Philip Caraman, head of the English Jesuits, was reminiscing about the writer Edith Sitwell: 'I was sitting with her at Paddington waiting for a train. It was at a time when Edith was having one of her skirmishes with Robert Conquest. There were a number of rasping announcements over the Tannoy. "I think," said Edith, "I will employ that gentleman to read Robert Conquest's poems."'

Mandrake, *Sunday Telegraph*, 4.8.85

\* \* \*

Sign in the window of a closed-down bookshop in New York: 'Words failed us'.

*Financial Times*, 31.10.86

\* \* \*

The best English diaries have been written by bores.

Kate O'Brien in *The Heritage of British Literature*

\* \* \*

Sir – Philip Howard (March 5) speculates about a relationship between the study of Latin and regular movement of the bowels (yes, bowels not vowels). The question has already been settled in respect of Greek by Dr John Armstrong MD in his metrical treatise *The Art of Preserving Health*:

29

> Read aloud resounding Homer's strain,
> And wield the thunder of Demosthenes,
> The chest so exercised improves
> And quick vibrations through the bowels drive
> The restless blood, which inactive days
> Would loiter else in inelastic tubes.

The digestive picture is a bit alarming but the purgative effect of Demosthenes is not in doubt.

Yours, etc., T J O Hickey

Letter to *The Times*, 9.3.87

Sir – Not only purgative (letter, March 9) but practical as well. Lord Chesterfield knew a gentleman who was so good a manager of his time that he would not even lose that small portion of it which the calls of nature obliged him to pass in the necessary house, but gradually went through all the Latin poets in those moments. He bought, for example, a common edition of Horace, of which he tore off gradually a couple of pages, carried them with him to that necessary place, read them first, and then sent them down as a sacrifice to Cloacina...

Yours, etc., Henry McDowell

Letter to *The Times*, 13.3.87

★ ★ ★

Those whom the Gods wish to destroy they first describe as 'promising'.
Christopher Hitchins reviewing *Cyril Connolly* by David Pryce-Jones, 22.7.83, page 23

★ ★ ★

There is a splinter of ice in the heart of a writer.
Graham Greene

★ ★ ★

Tristan Bernard, the French playwright and novelist, was sent a play to read by a young dramatist and asked for suggestions for a title. Bernard, not having read the play, asked the playwright, 'Are there any trumpets in your play?' 'No,' answered the puzzled young man. 'Are there any drums?' 'No.' 'Then why not call your play *Without Drums or Trumpets*?'

From *Book of Anecdotes*, 1985

\* \* \*

Few books of merit and importance have been composed either in a garret or a palace.

Edward Gibbon, *Memoirs*

\* \* \*

What progress we are making. In the Middle Ages they would have burned me. Nowadays they are content with burning my books.

Sigmund Freud to Ernest Jones about his books being burnt by the Nazis

\* \* \*

Of all the novels I've read, *Wuthering Heights* is the one I'd least like to be a character in.

Lewis Carroll

\* \* \*

I know no person so perfectly disagreeable and even dangerous, as an author.

Prince Regent

\* \* \*

George Mikes, Hungarian humorist, was planning to write a

book about psychiatry and decided that as a matter of research, he should experience a session of psychoanalysis. On the couch, the first question the psychiatrist put to him was, 'Did you have a happy childhood?' 'I'm still having one,' replied Mikes.

* * *

My sharpest memory of Basil Boothroyd is, suitably, of my being given a lesson in humour by him. I had been reading a book of his on public speaking which contains many wonderful stories, including one about a manicurist which Robert Robinson retells from time to time on radio. The best of all was a long tale about a disastrous trip to Lancashire during which Basil lost his speech notes and clothes because the train was divided at Crewe; made a doomed speech because the venue was an L-shaped room and he was in the short bit of the L; and found himself staying that night at quite the wrong address. Take it from me, it was hilarious to read. Next time I saw him, I begged him to tell me if it had all really happened.

'Miles,' he said, 'a professional humorist should know better than to ask questions like that. But as you're a mate, I'll tell you. Yes, it did really all happen. But not in that precise order... and not all on the same day... and not all to me.' And that is what humour is all about. Actually, it's what writing is all about.

Miles Kington, *Independent*, 2.3.88

* * *

Basil Boothroyd was probably the most professional writer I have ever known; and consequently both the most self-punishing and the least self-satisfied. Few have worked harder to make a sentence right, or to conceal the effort that had made it so, few have truffled longer or deeper in our bottomless vocabulary for the one word which would corral the elusive

32

thought, and very few indeed have sat like him, staring at a typed semi-colon for half an hour and deliberating whether or not a full colon might produce a more effective pause. Then coming back two hours later and making it a comma.

Once, on one of the very rare occasions when a piece I had commissioned from him did not come, he sent instead, without a covering note, a packet containing some three dozen foolscap sheets on each of which was typed the number 3. Most of them had a single word at the top; some had a syllable; a few only an inaugural letter or two. In the whiteness, you could feel the agony.

But on a good day, his sentences rang like struck crystal; and on the best days, they were as funny as anyone's have ever been.

Alan Coren, *The Times*, 2.3.88, pages 9–10

\* \* \*

29 March 1898 – Joseph Conrad writes to Edward Garnett: 'I sit down religiously every morning. I sit down for eight hours every day – and the sitting down is all. In the course of that working day of eight hours I write three sentences which I erase before leaving the table in despair...Sometimes it takes all my resolution and power of self-control to refrain from butting my head against the wall. I want to howl and foam at the mouth but I daren't do it for fear of waking the baby and alarming my wife. It's no joking matter. After such crises of despair I doze for hours, half conscious that there is a story that I am unable to write. Then I wake up, try again – and at last go to bed completely done-up. So the days pass and nothing is done. At night I sleep. In the morning I get up with the horror of that powerlessness that I must face through a day of vain efforts.'

Days Like This, *Independent*, 30.3.91

\* \* \*

If my books had been any worse I should not have been invited to Hollywood. If they had been any better, I should not have come.

Raymond Chandler, quoted by Godfrey Smith, *Sunday Times*, 6.3.88

★ ★ ★

Edith Sitwell's father told her she must do something distasteful every day. 'But I do, father,' she replied. 'I kiss you.'

Told by Sir Alec Guinness to Simon Callow, *The Times*, 12.5.88

★ ★ ★

Only a mediocre writer is always at his best.

Somerset Maugham

★ ★ ★

I certainly felt this when I was writing my recently published life of Tolstoy. You might think that the man who could describe Natasha Rostova's first ball would be sympathetic to women. You might even be simple-minded enough to suppose that the apostle of Peace and Love would have been able to create conditions of at least moderate harmony in his own home. In fact, having just penned some incredibly moving appeal to the peoples of the world to lay down their weapons and embrace universal brotherhood, he would be capable of bumping into his wife at the bottom of the stairs and saying, 'You poison the very air we breathe.'

A N Wilson, *Sunday Times*, 24.7.88

★ ★ ★

The following dedication appears in a book by a sociologist, Ken C. Kusterer, of the American University in Washington, *Know-How on the Job: The Important Working Knowledge of*

'Unskilled' Workers: 'To my family, to Faith and Jed and Todd. For four years my obsession with this project has dominated our family life. Like a malignant growth, "Daddy's work" has permeated every aspect of our relationships, taking over our vacations and wrecking our weekends. It seems almost a mockery to dedicate this, the cause of such pain, to you. But in this case, love means having to say it, in public print – I am sorry.'
Peter Simple, *Daily Telegraph*, 7.12.82

\* \* \*

George Orwell's independence rested on the discovery that those who live in glass houses were, after all, much the best qualified to throw stones.
Neal Ascherson reviewing *George Orwell* by T R Fyvel, *Observer*, 5.9.82

\* \* \*

Writers are usually in the unfortunate predicament of having to speak the truth without having the authority to speak it.
W H Auden

\* \* \*

> This author has got it made;
> No vestige of doubt now lurks.
> For consider this accolade:
> His books are known as Works

George Starbuck Galbraith

\* \* \*

Someone asked for a rare book at the Vatican Library. After about two hours a note came back: 'Missing since 1583.'
*Financial Times*, 5.4.88, page 16

\* \* \*

I think it was Graham Greene who said the only reason everyone thinks *Don Quixote* is such a wonderful book, is that nobody has ever read it. Anthony Burgess immediately swore that he had, but elsewhere the silence was deafening. Cross your heart and hope to die – have you read *Don Quixote*? All the way through...

I remember a seminar once where we were supposed to be discussing Richardson's novel, *Pamela*. Nobody, of course, had managed to finish it, and some had never even started. After some stilted discussion which centred mainly around the notes on the cover of the Penguin paperback, the professor turned to me and asked what I had made of the death of Northrop in the penultimate chapter. Safely, I thought, I told him that it had been 'very finely drawn'.

'Funny,' said the professor. 'No such character as Northrop is in *Pamela*.'

Martyn Harris, *Daily Telegraph*, 29.7.88, page 15

\* \* \*

When you have written four books, people begin to comment on your style. They have compared my bleak, chiselled style with Hemingway, Lawrence (D H, thank God, not T E). Yes, they are my writers. For bleak passages I have also looked hard at *Hedda Gabler*. But I was a boy who, at the age of eight, sang 'The Stately Homes of England' to the wind-up gramophone. I sang 'Mad Dogs and Englishmen' in falsetto: after puberty, having an extra male hormone or two, I couldn't get my tongue around Dig...arig...arig...arig...arig...arig... adoo. For writers who want to write dialogue, I can recommend nothing better than the breakfast scene in *Private Lives*.

Of course, I longed to meet the Master – and did so. It was his last lunch party in London before he crept off to die in Jamaica. The hostess was Anne Fleming, widow of Ian. The other members of the cast were Merle Oberon, Lady Diana Cooper, myself and him. I laughed so much the grouse came down my nose. He and Lady Diana did a dialogue about how, in the 1920s, they appeared in Chicago, he in *The Vortex*, she in *The Miracle*. On the way out from lunch he said, 'I have very much enjoyed meeting you, but unfortunately, we will never meet again because very shortly I will be dead. But if you'll take one parting word of advice: Never let anything artistic stand in your way.'

I have always acted on this advice.

Bruce Chatwin, extract from *What Am I Doing Here?* (Cape, 1989), reprinted in the *Daily Telegraph*, 6.5.89

\* \* \*

In 1656 Pascal wrote: 'I have only made this letter rather long because I have not had time to make it shorter.'

\* \* \*

15 October 1896 – Arnold Bennett writes in his journal: 'Does there, I wonder, exist a being who has read all, or approximately all, that the person of average culture is supposed to have read, and that not to have read is a social sin? If such a being does exist, surely he is an old, a very old man, who has read steadily that which he ought to have read sixteen hours a day, from early infancy. I cannot recall a single author of whom I have read everything – even of Jane Austen. Then there are large tracts of Shakespeare, Bacon, Spenser, nearly all Chaucer, Congreve, Dryden, Pope, Swift, Sterne, Johnson, Scott, Coleridge, Shelley, Byron, Edgeworth, Ferrier, Lamb, Leigh Hunt, Wordsworth (nearly all), Tennyson, Swinburne, the Brontës, George Eliot, W Morris, George Meredith, Thomas Hardy, Savage Landor, Thackeray, Carlyle – in fact, every classical author and most good modern authors, which I have never even overlooked. A list of the masterpieces I have *not* read would fill a volume.'

Ian Irvine, *Independent*, 21.10.89

\* \* \*

My note about the split infinitive reminded one reader of a letter Raymond Chandler wrote in 1948 to the editor of the *Atlantic Monthly*, 'Would you convey my compliments to the purist who reads your proofs,' he wrote, 'and tell him or her that I write in a sort of broken-down patois which is something like the way a Swiss waiter talks, and that when I split an infinitive, God damn it, I split it so that it will stay split.' Well said; but then Chandler, a master of his craft, knew a split infinitive when he saw one; and used them when he saw fit. Not too many come into the world that way.

Godfrey Smith, *Sunday Times*, 4.3.90

\* \* \*

The romantic novelists Catherine Cookson and Barbara Cartland were overheard at a literary lunch discussing their work. 'I have written seventy-six novels,' said Miss Cookson. 'I have actually written three hundred and twenty-seven,' replied Miss Cartland. 'Oh, I didn't know that you'd written one every year,' said Miss Cookson.

\* \* \*

Novel writing is really a matter of coming to terms with your own squalor.

Frederic Raphael

\* \* \*

Writing a poem is like a short love affair; writing a short story like a long love affair; writing a novel like a marriage.

Amos Oz

\* \* \*

27 March 1894 – Chekhov writes to Lydia Mizinova: 'I am in

Yalta and at loose ends, very much so. The local aristocracy or whatever you call it is putting on *Faust* and I attend rehearsals, delight in gazing upon a regular flowerbed of charming black, red, flaxen and auburn heads, listen to singing and eat; I dine upon deep-fat-fried lamb, onion fritters and mutton chops with kasha in the company of the directress of the girls' school; I eat sorrel soup with well-born families; I eat at the pastry shop and at my own hotel as well. I go to bed at ten, get up at ten and rest after dinner, but still I am bored, sweet Lika. I am not bored because I don't have "my women" around, but because the northern spring is better than this one, and the thought that I must, that I am obliged to write, won't leave me a single instant. I must write, write and write. I am of the opinion that real happiness is impossible without idleness. My ideal is to be idle and love a plump young girl. My most intense pleasure is to walk or sit doing nothing; my favourite occupation is picking useless stuff (leaves, straw, and so on) and doing useless things. Meanwhile I am a literary man and must write, even here at Yalta.'
Ian Irvine, *Independent*, 31.3.90

* * *

According to the first volume of Bevis Hillier's biography of Betjeman, it was at about this time [when he was an undergraduate at Oxford] that the future Poet Laureate had a fling with W H Auden, during which Auden's servant discovered them together and had to be bribed £5 to keep quiet. Afterwards Auden claimed the experience was not worth the fiver.
Diary, *The Times*, 14.1.91

* * *

13 November 1860 – Charles Greville writes the final entry in the diary he kept for forty years: 'At the end of three months since I last wrote anything in this book I take my pen in hand to record my determination to bring this journal (which is no

journal at all) to an end. I have long seen that it is useless to attempt to carry it on, for I am entirely out of the way of hearing anything of the slightest interest beyond what is known to all the world. I therefore close this record without any intention or expectation of renewing it, with a full consciousness of the smallness of value or interest, and with great regret that I did not make better use of the opportunity I have had of recording something more worth reading.'

*Independent*, 13.1.92

* * *

S J Perelman said of Philip Roth, author of the masturbation classic, *Portnoy's Complaint*, 'Sure I'd like to meet the author. I just don't want to shake him by the hand.'

* * *

The comedienne, Victoria Wood says that when she finds herself in W H Smith's, she can't resist picking up Margaret Drabble's novels and looking at the last chapter to see what doesn't happen.

Sean French, *The Times*, 28.12.96

* * *

'How on earth does one explain madness and love in sober prose with dates attached?' cried Virginia Woolf in despair as she attempted to complete her *Life* of Roger Fry.

Magnus Linklater, *The Times*, 2.1.97

* * *

No doubt his heart is in the right place – in other words, in a place where it hardly matters.

Peter Ackroyd on Gore Vidal, review of *Pink Triangle*, *The Times*, 19.8.82

* * *

Bernard Shaw claimed that his dramatic talent consisted of taking 'The utmost trouble to find the right thing to say, and then to say it with the utmost levity.'

★ ★ ★

How, you might wonder, do you write a biography of someone who is just twenty years old and who has spent nineteen of those years in almost total obscurity? The answer is, with great difficulty.

Penny Junor in her biography of Princess Diana

★ ★ ★

Auberon Waugh does not like poets. While applying for a drinks licence for the Academy Club in Soho, the editor of the *Literary Review* was asked by the chairman of the magistrates what kind of people would be patronising the new venue. When Waugh responded that poets were absolutely banned, the JP's face lit up and the licence was issued on the spot.

But why such an extreme literary sanction? 'The reason poets were originally banned from the old Academy was partly that they could talk of nothing but themselves, partly that they never paid for their drinks and partly that all the pretty women fell in love with them.' Bron should rename his club the Dead Poets' Society.

Diary, *The Times*, 9.5.98

★ ★ ★

The *New Yorker* once tried to buy a chapter from my *Life of Jesus*. I was thrilled. A month before publication, I received a call from someone who said he was the 'fact checker' who wanted to make sure the article had been thoroughly 'lawyered'. He spoke as if writs could easily arrive from Pontius Pilate or Judas Iscariot any minute. I tried to explain that the New Testament, however venerable a collection of writings, does not contain any 'facts' in the modern sense of the word. It was a case, as in Stalin's show trials, of 'everything is true except the facts'. After more conversations like this, my extract never got published.

A N Wilson, *Evening Standard*, 10.7.98

# Places to Love and Loathe

*(Cities and Towns)*

London is the worst place in the world for a good woman to grow better in.

John Vanbrugh

\* \* \*

New York is not the centre of the goddam universe. I grant you it's an exciting, vibrant, stimulating, fabulous city, but it is not Mecca. It just smells like it.

*California Suite* by Neil Simon

\* \* \*

If you faint in the street in Rome, you'll lose your wallet. If you faint in the street in New York, fourteen people will step over you. If you faint in the street in London someone will loosen your tie and call an ambulance. If you faint in the street in Dublin, four people will move over to make room for you.

Alan Whicker in conversation with Henry Kelly, on *Kelly on Sunday*, 24.8.86

\* \* \*

The town [of Brighton] is so truly desolate that if one had a mind to hang oneself for desperation at being obliged to live in it, it would be difficult to find a tree on which to fasten the rope.

Samuel Johnson on Brighton in the 1770s

\* \* \*

Brighton abounds in singular, cosy and flavourful public houses. They harbour distinctive colonies of regulars, rich in finely honed opinions, gorgeous in quaint apparel, creatures of fixed and often peculiar habits, whose hieratic or courtly gestures rivet the eye – a cast of thousands. Here are ancient stand-up comics, chorus girl colleagues of 'Bertie', broken poets and roistering companions of Dylan, scribblers who once walked Fleet Street arm-in-arm with Hannen Swaffer, old boys and girls who knew Noël Coward and Constant and Osbert, exchanged blows with Roy Campbell, bought porter for Brendan Behan, were almost 'spotted' by Chaplin, worked in MI5 under 'The Admiral', valeted the Duke of Windsor, slept with Errol Flynn and knew exactly where to find Lucky Lucan, Martin Bormann and the Loch Ness Monster.

Paul Johnson on Brighton in 1982, *Daily Telegraph*, 18.9.82

\* \* \*

In the kitchen (of my rented apartment in Venice) reside a pair of pet goldfish in a blue-and-white china bowl. In the bottom of the bowl is a pile of five- and ten-lire pieces. That is all – no greenery, no algae, no scum. The water is clear and still. The fish are extremely pale, almost white, as though their colour had been bled from them, and very lethargic in their movements, not to say torpid. The Signora insisted the fish did not have to be fed; that was the principle of this aquarium. The coins generated some sort of chemical in the water and the fish lived on that...I am too cowardly to put the poor creatures out of their misery, which a square meal of fish food would almost certainly bring about. I do not wish to incur the Signora's wrath; in her brusque way, she has an affection for these fish which is based on their prodigious powers of survival. So I conclude that I had best leave them as they are and take them as an allegory on Venice, a society which lived in a bowl and drew its sustenance from the filth of lucre.

Mary McCarthy in *Venice Observed*

'What a city to sack!'
Marshal Blücher on seeing London for the first time

★ ★ ★

The shipping forecast is an evocative poem of wild nature for the Londoner. One of the great pleasures of London life is to lie in bed before dawn, and hear this smooth urban voice droning on about terrible violent weather in places like Viking and German Bight (it couldn't be German Bite, could it?) and Fastnet and Butt of Harris, and Rockall. You know that all you have to do is get up, walk the beagles round the Serpentine, and catch the Central Line to the word factory.
Philip Howard, *The Times*, 9.11.84

★ ★ ★

In New York you hardly ever see anyone attractive on the streets. All the elegant people are in cars and the only decorative characters on the sidewalks are the blacks.
Horst P Horst (American photographer), quoted by Drusilla Beyfus, *Vogue*, May 1987

★ ★ ★

New York is the capital of a country that does not exist.
Saul Bellow, quoted in *The Times*, 20.8.88, page 9

★ ★ ★

Liverpool is a kind of collision caused by the English trying to get out while the Irish are trying to get in.

Nancy Banks-Smith, *Guardian*, 6.10.81

★ ★ ★

Last week I went to Philadelphia, but it was closed.

W C Fields

★ ★ ★

Big Ben is like British Democracy. It's loveable, noisy and strikes every fifteen minutes.

Anon

★ ★ ★

G K Chesterton admired the bright lights of Broadway. 'Magnificent!' he said. 'If only one could not read.'

★ ★ ★

It really is the perfect holiday. I mean, the heat is intense, the garden lovely, the chair long and cool, the lime-juice at hand, a bathing pool there, if one wishes to splash, scenery, books, gramophones, pretty people – and above all, the sense that it is not going on too long.

Harold Nicolson about Somerset Maugham's place, the Villa Mauresque at Cap Ferrat on the Riviera, 4.8.38

★ ★ ★

The pleasures of Venice could be justly compared to 'eating an entire box of chocolate liqueurs at one go'.

Truman Capote, quoted by Christine Doyle, *Daily Telegraph*, 12.12.97, page 24

★ ★ ★

Jeffrey Bernard, Low-Life columnist on the *Spectator*, was urged by well-meaning friends to go on holiday. He was to leave the friendly purlieus of Soho for a restoring break in Portugal. Bernard viewed the prospect with gloomy misgiving. Whatever they said about Portugal, he concluded, and all its holiday charms, there was one fatal flaw in the plan. 'I shall be there,' and that would effectively scupper any chance of his enjoying it. How profoundly true. The perfect holiday would be the holiday from oneself: but it has not been invented yet.

Godfrey Smith, *Sunday Times*, 24.8.86

# You are What You Wear

(Clothes)

But two days ago, I was saved. Setting out on a thirty-mile journey to buy a nightdress, I stopped in a nearby village to get petrol and saw a little draper's shop. On impulse I went in.

'Do you happen to have any nightdresses?' I heard myself asking.

The woman behind the counter nodded. She put a ladder against some shelves, clambered up, withdrew a box, clambered down and put it in front of me. On its lid was written 'Nightdress'. She opened the box and took it out. I looked at it. After a moment I said: 'Is this the only one?'

'It is,' the woman said.

'No other colours?'

'None.'

'No other pattern?'

'No.'

'What about size?'

'It's a nightdress,' she said, mildly astonished. 'Fits all sizes.'

I thought of all the nightdresses in all the shops in all the towns, the blue, pink, black, white nightdresses cut low and high with lace and spots and flowers, of cotton and silk and satin and polyester mixes, elegant, modest, naughty, baby-doll for the slim, the small, the large, the tall.

'I'll have it,' I said.

The nightdress is undistinguished. It has a round neck, long sleeves, an uneven hem, a lot of peculiar squiggles in a rather nasty blue and I love it. It cost me nothing in time or energy or worry or thought and when I put in on I wasn't richer or poorer, happier or unhappier, less loved or more, better at my job or worse, nearer to God or further. I was me in a room in a nightie. Oh, bliss. How're they going to keep me down in Paree, now that I've seen the farm?

Jill Tweedie, *Guardian*, 19.8.86

\* \* \*

A London author (James Leasor) asked for a sword stick umbrella (now illegal) at James Smith & Sons (umbrella and stick stores). The counter assistant produced a long and sharp weapon. 'I do believe, sir,' he said, 'that you'll find you can get three dead men on this blade.'

Quentin Letts, *Daily Telegraph*, 23.10.97

\* \* \*

Dunn & Co. The name was perfectly expressive of the thing itself – so dull, so grey, so reassuring. You knew where you were with Dunn & Co. You were in virtually any large high street in Britain. You had pushed open the wood-and-brass door of a building whose external decoration was a cross between that of a non-conformist tabernacle and a prep school honours board. You were facing a dark counter beneath whose glass reposed some grey socks and some black socks and some brown socks, all neatly folded next to some rather short scarves, which were blue or black or brown, and some nice safe driving gloves with leather on the inside bits and white mesh through which your fingers could breathe.

In the window were hats of the same colour range, some of them slightly angled, one or two containing in their bands feathers which might have been jaunty if they had not been quite so small and brown. Behind the counter was a grey-haired man (always a man) who wore a grey suit and an expression of restrained servility.

Would sir like a blazer of navy blue, or a light blue cardigan, or even a yellow waistcoat? To be honest, no, sir wouldn't particularly like any of those things. But that was not the point about Dunn & Co. Men did not patronize it because they *liked* what it sold, but because they despised men who liked their clothes.

Dunn catered for the man who did not want to make a fuss, so long as he was able to keep up his respectability. If Dunn had ever diversified, it would have sold pipes and faithful dogs and faithful wives and membership of the Rotary Club. And, although it was obviously true that Dunn was old-fashioned, it never made the mistake of being old-fashioned in an interesting way. No student, however ingenious, could use its wares as the basis of some romantic revival and bring his smart friends along to ruin the premises for the regular customers. Dunn knew how to keep the even tenor of its way.

It had to go, of course. The New Man did not mind about respectability and he *did* mind about being noticed. So Dunn found a new man, a bright young Mr Calladine, who had probably never worn a flat cap or checked carpet slippers in his life, and he changed everything. The shops changed their name to George Arthur Dunn, which was thought funkier, and the decorators began to chuck out the heraldic shields, while the tailors sharpened the suits.

As night follows day, the business faltered. Now Dunn & Co is for sale.

Charles Moore, *Daily Telegraph*, 31.1.91

# It's a Funny World

*(Countries and Peoples)*

Reuters reported from Peking yesterday: 'A village Communist Party chief has been arrested and charged with illegally detaining seventy-two of his neighbours and having seventeen of them tortured after his bicycle bell was stolen, the New China News Agency said today.'

*Daily Telegraph*, 16.9.86, page 13

\* \* \*

After saving his roubles for many years a Russian went along to buy his first motor car. The order was taken and he paid his money.

'When can I collect it?' he asked nervously.

'In ten years from today, comrade,' he was assured.

'Yes, but will it be in the morning or the afternoon?' he persisted.

'Does it matter comrade?'

'Well, it does . . . the plumber is coming in the morning.'

Observer, *Financial Times*, 24.9.87

\* \* \*

In the West people make free with words like 'Freedom' and 'the Spirit' but few ever think of asking a man whether he has enough money for lunch.

Czeslaw Milusz in 'Visions from San Francisco Bay', *Spectator*, 4.12.82, page 23

\* \* \*

If an English butler and an English nanny sat down to design a country they would come up with New Zealand.

*Traveller's Dictionary of Quotations* (Chick)

★ ★ ★

The Soviet Union is the only country where the artist is held in such esteem that he is frequently put in prison to prevent him leaving.

Peter Ustinov, *Sunday Times*, 24.3.85

★ ★ ★

Australia is a huge rest home where no unwelcome news is ever wafted on to the pages of the worst newspapers in the world.

Germaine Greer, *Observer*, 1.8.82

★ ★ ★

The Soviet Union has closed the technology gap with the West according to a story from Helsinki. Ivan is trudging across Red Square with two heavy suitcases when his friend Sasha stops him to ask the time. Ivan rests the cases and looks at his watch.

'Three o'clock in Helsinki, 7.00 a.m. in New York, 9.00 p.m. in Tokyo. Wind west-south-west, and it should be a fine weekend.'

'Gosh,' says Sasha, 'I didn't know you could buy those fancy Japanese watches here.'

'What do you mean, Japanese? This is a Soviet watch. I've just bought it from GUM.'

'Colossal. I must get one.'

'You should,' says Ivan, as he picks up his two suitcases. 'But I warn you, these batteries don't half weigh you down.'

Observer, *Financial Times*, 28.6.85

I was not altogether surprised by the misfortunes which befell some of Mrs Thatcher's staff in Kano last week. Nigeria is a country where the unexpected very readily occurs. In 1959, Lord De La Warr, father of the present earl, Elwyn Jones and I flew to Kano to assist in celebrations marking independence for Northern Nigeria.

Many guests had been invited and we braced ourselves for a certain amount of confusion at Kano airport. There was none. Our reception, and in particular the handling of our baggage, compared most favourably with experience at most international airports today. On leaving the airport we warmly thanked the baggage wallah.

'We shall meet again tomorrow – in Parliament,' he replied cheerfully. 'I am also Mr Speaker.'

W F Deedes, *Daily Telegraph*, 11.1.88

\* \* \*

Israelis have one major regret about their homeland. 'Why didn't Moses turn right instead of left when he crossed the Red Sea,' they mutter, 'and then we'd have had the oil.'

\* \* \*

The French spend their lives in saving small fortunes. A Frenchman dreams of a smart funeral. He works hard throughout a lifetime to be able to die above his station.

George Mikes

\* \* \*

California is a fine place to live in – if you happen to be an orange.

Fred Allen (American radio comic)

\* \* \*

In Italy for thirty years under the Borgias they had warfare, terror, murder, bloodshed. They produced Michelangelo, Leonardo da Vinci and the Renaissance. In Switzerland they had brotherly love, five hundred years of democracy and peace and what did they produce? The cuckoo clock.

Orson Welles as Harry Lime in Graham Greene's script of *The Third Man*

\* \* \*

Canada — I don't even know which street it's on.

Al Capone

\* \* \*

Canada is all right really, though not for the whole weekend.

Saki, quoted in the *Independent*, 16.4.88, page 37

\* \* \*

In the Arab world a secret is a piece of information that has not yet been sold.

Quoted in profile of President Assad, *Independent*, 22.8.87, page 10

\* \* \*

A reporter who quotes his foreign taxi-driver is usually short of material but I am omitting my thoughts on the Chagall exhibition at the Beaubourg to honour the fellow who got my fare outside the ORTF building. He was straight out of Godard. To begin with, he'd just been listening to *France-Culture* on his radio and reckoned I hadn't given the anarchists of '68 enough credit. He then picked up a volume of Marx from the empty seat beside him. 'I study the historical dialectic in traffic jams.'

Passing the Opéra, he spoke with a passionate eloquence, his left hand very active, about Socrates ('the first true anarchist') and Descartes ('the French people today lack Cartesian rigour'). From there he passed to Marx's argument with Proudon ('property is theft'), denounced Le Pen for racism, and dismissed Socialist Party politicians as *plus royaliste que le roi*. I studied my taxi-driver unbelievingly all the way to Charles de Gaulle airport: he had a fantastic Tarzan profile but a soft, defeated look when he turned to smile.

David Caute, *Independent*, 2.6.88

\* \* \*

Four condemned men – a Frenchman, Englishman, American and German – facing a firing squad were asked to state their final wish. The Frenchman wanted to sing the *Marseillaise* and then was shot. The Englishman asked for a cup of tea and then was shot. The German asked if he could make a statement explaining the overall concept of European security and federation. On hearing this the American asked if his final wish could be that he be shot before the German.

*Financial Times*, 17.1.97

\* \* \*

Sir – May I put in a word for the brevity of the English language. In a golf club in Spain I noticed on the door leading from the course to the bar the following written request: *El Secretario y la Junda de este Club notifica a los miembros e invitados que han estado jugando al golf y que desean usar el bar que deberan quitarse los zapatos de golf antes en entrar en este recinto para evitar destrozar la moqueta. Se agradece la cooperacion de los miembros a este respecto.*

Underneath it said in English: No spikes.

John Clarke, Oakham, Rutland

\* \* \*

That aphorism about heaven and hell echoes round the world. In California, they say heaven is an English house, a Chinese cook, an American salary and a Japanese wife. Hell for them is a Japanese house, an English cook, a Chinese salary and an American wife. The Japanese, on the other hand, say heaven is a Western house, a Japanese wife, a Chinese cook and a French mistress. What Japanese women think we don't know. One of these days perhaps they'll tell us.

Godfrey Smith, *Sunday Times*, 13.1.91

★ ★ ★

Francis Bacon said of Switzerland, 'One bloody picture postcard after the other. Nothing but views.'

Jeffrey Bernard, *Spectator*, 17.8.96

★ ★ ★

A Pole was having his eyes tested. The doctor asked him to look at the bottom line of his eye chart, which contained the letters 'ZYLKXOSKI'. 'Can you read it?' asked the doctor. 'Can I read it?' replied the Pole, 'he's my cousin.'

★ ★ ★

A Japanese went to have his eyes examined. 'You have a cataract,' said the eye specialist. 'No, I have a Rincoln Contirental,' said the Japanese.

★ ★ ★

Two Africans walking past a tall tree, spotted a man at the top gibbering and making mad and violent gestures. 'He's been whiteballed at Black's,' says one spectator to the other.

★ ★ ★

In Europe they name a street after you one day and chase you down it the next.
Arthur Baer

* * *

I used to hate the French but after living there for a long time I have begun to like them. But I like them for the wrong reasons. They are so selfish that they never care about anyone else, are never interested in anyone else. If they pass me in the street and one of them says, 'Oh, that's Omar Sharif!' the other will say, 'So what, who cares?' That's fine for somebody like me because it means they never stare at you or ask you for autographs and they leave you alone. The other thing I like about the French is that they are such bad actors in their private lives. They always reveal their true feelings about you on their faces. You know that they either hate you or dislike you. If they do smile at you, then you know they really like you.
Omar Sharif on *The Terry Wogan Show*, BBC, 16.4.83

* * *

Whenever I'm in a group of white intellectuals, I have a method for discovering the racists. I talk nonsense, utter unqualified rubbish. I then support it with theories of the most grotesquely absurd nature. If the whites around me listen with respect and at the end overwhelm me with applause and praise, I have no doubt! They're racist pigs.
James Baldwin quoted by Conor Cruise O'Brien, *Observer*, 3.6.84, page 7

* * *

Two African natives were discussing the quality of the missionary they had just eaten for dinner. Said one, 'Better than that muck we used to get at the London School of Economics.'

* * *

I visited the Arizona State Penitentiary where eighty per cent of the prisoners are black. What's strange about that is there ain't no black people in Arizona.

Richard Pryor (actor), playing black comic on Sunset Strip (film)

* * *

I've just been to Africa, I tell you Tarzan wouldn't last a week there.

Ibid.

* * *

I have no malice. I've helped the Indian Flood Relief, the Jewish National Home...I believe all the Jews, Catholics, Methodists, Protestants should get together...and attack the Pakistanis.

Bernard Manning (north country comedian), 1980

* * *

If a Japanese is too logical, he is considered very funny, my friend Hata-san tells me in Tokyo. This insight may help some of the more miserable English dealers floundering around in Japan this week.

'Our language is very ambivalent,' says Hata-san, recalling with pleasure a recent American judgement that Japanese are liars. 'Only we understand its connotations. If I say, "I do my very best," that means, "No way do I do it." If I say, "I shall make efforts," that is the polite way to say, "I shall try to not succeed." If I say, "I will think about it," it means, "Almost a hundred per cent No."'

What about 'Hai' and 'Iiye'? 'Hai', says Hata-san, means more like sixty per cent Yes, forty per cent No. 'Iiye' the reverse. 'Ambiguity is part of Japanese culture. Our language is no good for science or mathematics but very good for politics.

We are a sneaky race,' he adds disarmingly. No one could think so, I reply, but he insists.

'Did you know that Japanese are seventy-five per cent Shintoists and seventy-five per cent Buddhists?' I am lost, but for Hata-san this is proof that compromise lies at the heart of every Japanese opinion. 'Shintoism says that drinking is OK, but Buddhism does not like it. So I am a Buddhist by day and a Shintoist after dark. If I get drunk, next morning I repent. Do you follow?'

Godfrey Barker, *Daily Telegraph*, 28.5.90

\* \* \*

The Oxford University Press has reduced its Oxford books to absurdity, with the *Oxford Book of Canadian Political Anecdotes*. In any catalogue of short books this must hold its own with *Great Argentine Victories, Ayatollah Khomeini's Ecumenical Service Book, The Robert Maxwell Diet* and *The Wit and Wisdom of the Oxford University Press*.

Christopher Fildes, *Spectator*, 25.2.89

\* \* \*

On the eve of celebrations for the two hundredth anniversary of the storming of the Bastille, BBC *Breakfast TV* discussed the royalist faction in France, suggesting the return of the monarchy.

'Do you think the French believe in the monarchy?' a Frenchman was asked by the BBC interviewer.

His reply: 'I do not think the French believe in anything that lasts too long – except lunch.'

*Breakfast TV*, 13.7.89

\* \* \*

The imbalance between ideals and ideology, and the horrific

reality that may arise from it, is the French philosopher Bernard-Henri Levy's raw material. Listening to Levy it appears that French intellectualism emerged more than anything from military defeat, something of which the French have some experience.

I recently had a particularly irate letter from an English reader who abused the French in every way he could think of, but especially and bizarrely for what he imagined to be their capacity to get over things, to forget the skeletons in the national closet. How he asked can one possibly respect people who could put behind them such appalling events as the Nazi occupation and the Vichy collaboration?

The truth is, of course, that they have not forgotten them at all: they are discussed and reinterpreted and agonized over constantly – by the intellectuals.

The France of liberty and ideals is pitted daily against the France of self-saving willingness to compromise; the penchant for fascism, racism and materialism against the grand republican notions and an almost touching faith in humanitarianism.

The man of action de Gaulle (who was of course an *intellectual* man of action) weighs against the thinker – Sartre again, perhaps, viewing things from the sidelines in the Café de Flore.

Suzanne Lowry, *Daily Telegraph*, 22.3.91

* * *

Even in the middle of a revolution, the Parisian crowd kept a sense of humour. Camille Desmoulins, who became one of the most popular journalists in Paris, reported this in a letter to his father.

'A few days ago one of the orators of the biggest crowd concluded with this motion: "Let's burn down the house of M. d'Eprémesnil, his wife, his children, his furniture and the man himself." That was about to be carried unanimously, when

60

someone said: "Gentlemen, d'Eprémesnil's upholsterer demands to speak." They shouted: "Let the upholsterer speak." "Gentlemen," said the honourable member, "I demand grace for d'Eprémesnil's furniture, which belongs to me since he has not paid me a sou for it." "That's fair," shouts the assembly. The upholsterer thanked them. "Gentlemen, since you have respected the fairness of my request, may I put in a word for the absent M.–, the architect, who built d'Eprémesnil's house, which doesn't belong to him since he hasn't paid for it..." Everyone shouted in favour of the architect, "Pardon for the house!" "As for his wife," resumed the upholsterer, "why do you want to burn your own property? You know his wife is public property, and belongs to everybody, and is it not possible that several of you know that only too well? So pardon for Madame! And if you were to burn his children would you not be afraid of committing the crime of Oedipus – involuntary parricide?" "Yes, yes!" they shouted, "Pardon for the wife and the children!"

"'As for the man himself, gentlemen, I won't stop you burning him, either in person or in effigy." The funniest thing about the anecdote is that I am assured that it was M. d'Eprémesnil himself who proposed the motion.'

\* \* \*

Being a Canadian means more than playing hockey and objecting to being called an American.

Nicholas R M Lowson in a letter to the *Financial Times*, 2.3.93

\* \* \*

Georgy Plakhanov, the veteran Russian Marxist, was asked in 1918 what had been the chief characteristic of his people's long and colourful history. After giving the matter a great deal of mature consideration, he replied: 'They steal.'

Norman Stone, reviewing *A People's Tragedy* by Orlando Figes, *Sunday Times*, 18.8.96

Stone added at the end of his review: 'Russians still steal, unfortunately, and have been doing so fairly comprehensively from the World Bank and other such well-meaning institutions, to pursue their bizarre war against the Chechens.'

\* \* \*

British comedy does not always amuse others. Vernon Lawrence, head of comedy at Yorkshire Television, recalls watching a British programme at Montreux with a top West German comedy director. 'There was a sketch involving a street cleaner – you saw him sweep out the gutter, look around to see if anyone was watching and then lift up the pavement and sweep the rubbish underneath. The German was absolutely stone-faced. He said he couldn't see the joke, because in Germany you can't lift up the pavement.'
Patrick Stoddard, *Sunday Times*, 14.5.89

\* \* \*

Last week's *Spectator* contains an article by Sir Charles Powell, Lady Thatcher's former policy adviser, about the historic rivalry between Britain and France. He wonders if it will ever end, recalling General de Gaulle saying that 'fundamentally our two countries have always been at war'.

I am reminded of an incident many years ago in Paris when I deviously nipped into a parking place which a French driver had earmarked for himself in Rue Berthollet on the Left Bank. My Mini had a British number plate, and when I came back to reclaim it, I found a notice under the windscreen wiper. It listed almost every humiliation we have inflicted on the French – Crécy, Poitiers, Agincourt, Waterloo, Mers-el-Kebir and so on – and ended: '... *et maintenant, Rue Berthollet.*'

Unless the French start forgetting their history there will be little chance for the reconciliation for which Sir Charles hopes.
Alexander Chancellor, *Daily Telegraph*, 6.9.94

I once questioned a friend who had spent a good deal of time in India in connection with some industrial concern, and asked him what India was really like. He thought for a bit and then answered: 'It is like Ashton-under-Lyne, only hotter!' And the photographs he produced, which were principally of the interiors of cotton mills in Bombay, bore out his statement remarkably well. I asked him about the natives and he said: 'After a time you don't notice them.'

James Agate, *Around Cinemas*, 1935

\* \* \*

I agree with the German professor who once said, 'If a man will be born an Armenian, he should know what to expect.'

Ibid., p.32

\* \* \*

The Jews invented guilt and the Irish turned it into an art form.

Walter Matthau in Jonathan Green's *Says Who?*

\* \* \*

An Irish drunk staggered towards two nuns in the street and they separated to let him pass. Once past him they came together again. Puzzled, the drunk stared back at their retreating figures. 'How did she do that?' he mused.

\* \* \*

Irish drunk trying to make an obscene phone call: 'Madam, I'm trying to shock and disgust you. Will you please stop telling me the time.'

Larry Adler, 2.7.82

\* \* \*

A rich Irish woman refused a local anaesthetic because she could afford something better.

* * *

An Irish queen is a man who prefers women to Guinness

* * *

MacGregor, Goldberg and Kelly were on holiday together in Rome and were told by reliable Vatican sources that the Pope would be dead in two weeks. They agreed that this sure thing was a bet worth having when they got back to London. As predicted the Pope duly died within two weeks, and the three friends met to tell each other how they had done with their wagers.

'I did very well,' said MacGregor. 'I got five hundred to one at Ladbroke's.'

'I did better than that,' said Goldberg. 'I got seven hundred to one at William Hill's.'

They then turned to Kelly and asked him how his bet had gone. 'Oh, I lost,' said Kelly.

'But how could you have? asked his astonished friends.

'I had a double with the Archbishop of Canterbury.'

Anon

* * *

Judge: You have been found not guilty by a Limerick jury and you leave this court with no other stain on your reputation.

* * *

The Irish are a fair people: they never speak well of one another.

Samuel Johnson (1709–84)

* * *

I have never heard a thousand bagpipes before. Nobody has. Some in bearskins and some in bonnets, all with swelling calves in straining socks, each with a sort of octopus tucked under his arm... It's an odd thing but a thousand bagpipers are no worse – if I may put it like that – than one. The noise does not seem to get any louder, only more edgy and irritable like live tinned bees. As the Duke of Wellington said: 'I don't know what they do to the enemy but I think I'll go and lie down for a bit.'

Nancy Banks-Smith, TV review of the opening of the Commonwealth Games in Edinburgh, *Guardian*, 26.7.86

\* \* \*

Of Scotsmen, Sydney Smith said: 'It requires a surgical operation to get a joke well into a Scotchman's head. Their only idea of wit is laughing immoderately at stated intervals.'

*Telegraph*, June 1994

\* \* \*

Mr Simcha Dinitz, formerly the Israeli ambassador to Washington and now chairman of the Jewish Agency and World Zionist Organization, was reminiscing about the confused perceptions of his job. During his tenure in Washington he recalled being summoned at 11 p.m. to the Pentagon by a worried James Schlesinger, then Defense Secretary, who was deeply concerned about Jewish reaction to remarks made by the chairman of the chiefs of staff, General Brown, during an off-the-record speech.

The remarks that Jews controlled the American media, industry and banks, had been leaked to the press and the next day's newspapers were headlining them. Could Mr Dinitz please make sure that Jewish reaction to this was muted, since the chairman really didn't mean what he said, was definitely a friend of Israel's and the Administration didn't want to have to fire him.

Mr Dinitz explained that he had no special influence over American Jewry. But as instructed he went back to his embassy and sent out a telex to the eight Israeli consulates in the US. The telex read: 'Tomorrow, you will read in *The New York Times* and *Washington Post* that Jews control the media, industry and banks. Deny, but not too vehemently.'
Barbara Amiel, *The Times*, 22.3.88

\* \* \*

A Jewish boy went with Stanley Reynolds and his son to see *Hamlet* for the first time. On leaving, his sole comment on the play was, 'A boy shouldn't talk to his mother like that.'
Stanley Reynolds

\* \* \*

'If I see something I like, I buy it; then I try to sell it.'
Lord Lew Grade (British impresario)

\* \* \*

When Pierre Monteux the French conductor was seriously ill and had not long to live he was baptized and became a Catholic. Asked why he had made such a decision on what was virtually his deathbed, he replied, 'I do not want another Jew to die.'

\* \* \*

There is always the danger in Judaism of seeing history as a sort of poker game played between Jews and God, in which the presence of others is noted but not given much importance.
Rabbi Lionel Blue, *Observer*, 29.8.82

# They Slit a Nightingale's Throat
### (Critics)

Don't be afraid of criticism. Anyone who can fill out a laundry slip thinks of himself as a writer. Those who can't fill out a laundry slip think of themselves as critics.
George Seaton

★ ★ ★

The fate of critics is to be remembered by what they failed to understand.
George Moore

★ ★ ★

A B Walkley was *The Times* great dramatic critic. He wrote very quickly, very elegantly: a man of the world. He came back one night to his room to write his notice of the play he had seen. You could run up to 2 a.m. in those days. But this night he was running late, so the chief sub-editor sent a messenger to ask whether Walkley would mind parting with his copy a sheet at a time. He agreed and sent it down sheet by sheet. On the last sheet he wrote that he could not do justice to the play, because fire had broken out, and the last act had never been given. On the following day, editor Geoffrey Dawson wrote him an old-fashioned *Times* letter: 'Dear Mr Walkley, it would have been of the greatest convenience to *The Times* if, on your coming into the office from the play last night, you had taken the trouble to mention that the theatre was on fire.' Walkley wrote back at once: 'Dear Mr Editor, you mistake my

employment. I am your drama critic, not your newshawk.'
William Lawrence, *The Times*, 2.1.85

★ ★ ★

The first duty of a dramatic critic is to learn to sleep sitting
upright and without anybody noticing.
William Archer, quoted in *Around Cinemas* by James Agate, op. cit., page 20

★ ★ ★

James Agate was called in to his editor's office and told that
there had been a complaint from the management of the play
he had reviewed in that morning's paper. 'They tell me,' said
the editor, 'that you were asleep during most of the third act
and that you couldn't possibly have been able to make a fair
assessment of the play.' 'Sleep,' replied Agate, 'is also an aspect of
criticism.'

★ ★ ★

They search for ages for the wrong word which, to give them
credit, they eventually find.
Peter Ustinov, *The Critics*, BBC Radio, 1952

★ ★ ★

A critic is one who has been given a pass-key into many rooms
in the House of Arts on condition that he does not dwell in any
of them. His part is to open a door, examine the furniture of the
room, and compare the view from its window with those to be
seen from others. He must stay long enough to see what the
owner of the room saw – then he had better move on.
Desmond MacCarthy, quoted in David Cecil's *MacCarthy, His Writings*

★ ★ ★

My first short story was harshly denounced by one particular critic. I brooded and made caustic remarks about the man. Then one day I reread the story and realized he had been correct. It was shallow and badly constructed. I never forgot the incident and years later, when the Luftwaffe were bombing London, I shone a light on the critic's house.

W. Somerset Maugham, quoted by Miles Kington, *The Times*, June 1981

★ ★ ★

The editor of the *Evening Standard* called me into his office and rebuked me for having written in a first-night notice that the play had been so bad I had not come back after the interval for the third act. 'You are paid to stay,' he sternly informed me.

Milton Shulman

★ ★ ★

A dismal evening: fight to get rid of tickets.

Rodney Milne, reviewing *Carmen* at Royal Opera House, *Evening Standard*, 29.4.91

★ ★ ★

Being a drama critic was like being the eternal diner in somebody else's restaurant: you never get to choose the menu or rewrite the wine list.

Ken Tynan to Sheridan Morley, *Spectator*, 8.8.92

★ ★ ★

When Sir Harold Hobson, long-time theatre critic of the *Sunday Times*, met French playwright Genet, he said, 'Je suis critic, M. Genet.' To which the playwright replied, 'Et moi, M. Hobson. Je suis pederast.'

★ ★ ★

When Hobson interviewed Bernard Shaw at his home, Eyot St Lawrence, in the 1940s Shaw said, 'Have you come all this way to ask me those silly questions?' 'Yes,' said Hobson. 'Then you'd better get back as quickly as possible,' said Shaw.

*An Important Journey* by Sir Harold Hobson

★ ★ ★

A friend of mine's a critic who's changed into a gull
And though his life is brighter, his writing now seems dull
For while his methods altered, he never lost his flair:
What he did on paper, he now does from the air.

Simon Drew, in a publicity handout for the Antique Collectors Club in Woodbridge, Suffolk

★ ★ ★

At the beginning of the nineteenth century theatrical criticism was completely venal and lunchable. Hacks got free tickets and lunch, and in return published puffs, often written by the actors or the dramatists themselves. The first candid theatre critic, Leigh Hunt, described the racket: 'What the public took for a criticism of a play was a draft upon the box-office or reminiscences of last Thursday's salmon and lobster sauce.'

John Walter II, the admirable young man who was becoming the founding father of a free press, instructed theatre critics of *The Times* to pay for their own tickets, to give up lunch and to write an honest criticism of the play. This they did with some gusto: 'Utterly contemptible...ceaseless scribbler...insipid songs and nauseous courtesies...Mr Cherry is undoubtedly the lowest dramatist of this wretched day.'

The theatrical managers and actors were outraged. *The Times* had treacherously stabbed them in their most tender parts: the purse and the lunch. But *The Times* was right. It is a silly as well as an offensive suggestion that lunch can influence a man's opinion.

Philip Howard, *The Times*, 3.8.84

★ ★ ★

After the first night of a musical called *Troubadour*, which was heavily backed by Japanese money, Sheridan Morley began his first night notice: 'First, Pearl Harbor and now this...'

* * *

Book reviewing is a whole-time job with a half-time salary. A job in which our best work is always submerged in the criticism of someone else's, where all triumphs are ephemeral and only the drudgery is permanent and where no future is secure except the certainty of turning into a hack.

Philip Larkin's introduction to a new edition of Cyril Connolly's *The Condemned Playground*, *Sunday Times*, 24.2.85

* * *

My own attitude to critics is clear and entirely reasonable. It is one of distrust and dislike based on predictability and historical fact. I regard them as something like kinky policemen on the cultural protectionist make, rent collectors, screws, insurance men, customs officers and fairground showmen. One should simply not open one's door to them.

John Osborne in *Sunday Telegraph*, 1966. (Subsequently, Osborne frequently reviewed plays and films and was regular TV critic for the *Mail on Sunday*, June to August 1982.)

* * *

The fact is, though nobody has perceived it, that a professional play critic is a monstrosity – a sow with five legs or a man with four thumbs. Nature did not intend him, and that is why we have to conceal our repulsion when he confronts us.

Clifford Bax, quoted by James Agate

* * *

It was one of those plays in which all the actors unfortunately enunciated very clearly.
Robert Benchley

* * *

Asking a working writer what he feels about critics is like asking a lamp-post what it feels about dogs.
John Osborne

* * *

I am sitting in the smallest room of my house. Your notice is before me. It will shortly be behind me.
Noël Coward to a critic who had savaged one of his plays

* * *

A critic is a person who will slit the throat of a skylark to see what makes it sing.
Irish playwright, quoted by Colin Welland on *Quote, Unquote*, BBC Radio 4

* * *

Here she comes! Just the same dear little face − except that now there's another dear little face all around it.
James Agate, about an ageing actress

* * *

Take heed of critics, they bite, like fish, at anything.
Thomas Dekker

* * *

Tom Stoppard, asked in a TV programme what Ken Tynan had

contributed to the theatre, said, 'He made it worthwhile trying to be good.'
July 1982

★ ★ ★

The smiling sewing machine.'
Yeats of Shaw

★ ★ ★

He is every other inch a gentleman.
Rebecca West

★ ★ ★

I have no wish to know anyone sitting in a sewer and adding to it.
Carlyle writing about Swinburne, quoted by Taki, *Spectator*, 27.8.83

★ ★ ★

Diana Vreeland, long-time editor of American *Vogue*, was not always popular with her staff and associates. She once asked a *Vogue* colleague, 'What is the name of that designer who hates me so?' Replied the colleague, 'Legion.'
Jeremy Campbell, *Evening Standard*, 6.6.84

★ ★ ★

When the TV executive Donald Baverstock was replaced at the BBC by Huw Wheldon, the TV producer Ned Sherrin was summoned for an interview. 'It was quite astonishing,' wrote Sherrin, 'everything from Baverstock's office had been removed overnight; the office was quite completely bare. So I said to Huw, "Ah, I see you've put the stamp of your personality on the office."'
*Sunday Times*, 26.8.84

★ ★ ★

Spike Milligan put his house in North London on the market early in 1987. When the estate agent asked him if he had any objection to a Japanese purchaser, Spike said he was perfectly happy for him to have the house – with one proviso, that it should be wired up to explode on the anniversary of Pearl Harbor.

Richard Ingrams, *Independent*, 15.4.88

★ ★ ★

The only thing moving about Charlton Heston's performance was his wig.

Michael Coveney

★ ★ ★

I'm enormously attached to people who aim low... and miss.

Peter Ustinov, *Daily Mail*, 17.10.90, page 32

# Money Talks

*(Economics and Money)*

An economics student who returned to his university after twenty years found, to his astonishment, that the examination questions were exactly the same as the ones he was faced with in his time. 'Ah yes,' said his old professor. 'You see in economics the questions stay the same but we change the answers.'

William Davis, *Guardian*, 8.1.70

★ ★ ★

Home is where the mortgage is.

Billy Connolly

★ ★ ★

It is hard to be without money. To get on without it is like travelling in a foreign country without a passport – you are stopped, suspected, and made ridiculous at every turn, besides being subjected to the most serious inconveniences.

William Hazlitt, quoted in the *Spectator*, 10.9.83, page 24

★ ★ ★

A man who visited London's casinos for an occasional gamble received the following letter from his bank manager:

Dear —— ,
I note that at the close of yesterday's business your account was again overdrawn considerably beyond the limit recently agreed between ourselves.

I note, furthermore, that in the past three weeks we have honoured several cheques for substantial sums made payable to the Clermont Club. I understand that this is a gaming establishment in Mayfair.

As a result I must therefore ask whether you could help me to become a member of the Clermont Club.

Yours, etc . . .

*Mail on Sunday*, 1.7.84, page 9

\* \* \*

Practical men, who believe themselves to be quite exempt from any intellectual influences, are usually the slaves of some defunct economist.

John Maynard Keynes, *General Theory*

\* \* \*

The doorman at the London Hilton Hotel was greeted by a Texan oil billionaire with the words: 'What's the biggest tip you've ever received?' The doorman replied, '£14,000, sir.' The Texan, saying he did not wish to be outdone, presented him with £20,000 on the spot. As he turned to go the Texan asked the doorman: 'Mind telling me who gave you the £14,000?' The doorman replied: 'You did, sir.'

Lady Olga Maitland, *Sunday Express*, 3.7.83

\* \* \*

Nubar Gulbenkian, the Armenian multi-millionaire, used to ride around London in a custom-built replica of a London taxi. His explanation for using such an eccentric vehicle was because 'I was told it will turn on a sixpence – whatever that may be.'

James Cameron, *Guardian*, 18.1.83

\* \* \*

During the slump in the Stock Market in London, a question was asked: 'How do you become a millionaire in the Stock Market?' The answer came: 'By starting with two million.'
July 1985

\* \* \*

> That money talks
> I'll not deny
> I heard it once,
> It said 'Goodbye.'

Anon

\* \* \*

Happiness is the deferred fulfilment of a prehistoric (pre-adult) wish. That is why wealth brings so little happiness; money is not an infantile wish.
Sigmund Freud, 16 January 1898

\* \* \*

J Paul Getty, American oilman, was asked by a reporter if it was true that his wealth, at that time, amounted to a billion dollars. 'I suppose so,' he said, 'but remember, a billion dollars doesn't go as far as it used to.'
Clifton Fadiman (ed.), *Faber Book of Anecdotes*

\* \* \*

Alexander Woolcott, critic and broadcaster, on visiting the playwright Moss Hart's sumptuous mansion with its elaborate landscaped grounds, said, 'Just what God would have done if he had had the money.'
Ibid.

\* \* \*

Not even love can make so many fools of men as the pondering over the nature of money.

William Ewart Gladstone during a debate on Peel's Bank Act 1844–5, quoted by William Rees-Mogg, *Independent*, 23.10.89, page 21

★ ★ ★

Bob Hope thought that news of his having four hundred million dollars would ruin his career. No one would laugh at so rich a man.

Dick Cavett, speaking on CNN *Crossfire* on 15.1.93

★ ★ ★

Economists belong to the one profession where you can gain great eminence without ever being right.

George Meaney, US trade union leader

★ ★ ★

A cartoon shows a man selling matches on Wall Street wearing a sign around his neck saying: 'I'm here on expert advice.'

★ ★ ★

Lord (Lew) Grade was once told by his wife to cheer himself up and go to America and sell something.

★ ★ ★

There are two times in a man's life when he should not speculate: when he can't afford it, and when he can.

Mark Twain

# Learning is a Dangerous Thing
### *(Education)*

Lord Berners, who had been far from happy at his prep school, decided years later to pay the school a visit. All was as he remembered, except the atmosphere – full of a new cheerfulness and gaiety that had been missing. He found it was a school no longer and had become a private lunatic asylum.

Arthur Marshall in *Whispering in the Rhododendrons*, who comments: 'Some will find this less peculiar than others.' *Daily Telegraph*, 9.9.82, page 15

\* \* \*

A professor is one who talks in someone else's sleep.

W H Auden

\* \* \*

At an oral examination at Oxford, known as a viva, a candidate was asked, 'What is electricity?' Woefully unprepared, the youth stammered: 'Oh dear, sir. I remember quite distinctly knowing the answer – but I am afraid I have forgotten it.' 'How very unfortunate,' replied the examiner. 'Until today only two people knew what electricity was – you and the Author of Nature, and now you have forgotten it.'

\* \* \*

Q   At school we used to recite a mock Latin poem which began:

Caesar adsum iam forte
Brutus aderat
Caesar sic in omnibus
Brutus ...

How did the poem end, and are there any more such joke Latin poems?

A   'Brutus in isat'. According to Nigel Molesworth (1953), 'all latin masters hav one joke' and that's it. Molesworth also notes that 'a good roare of larffter will cut the leson by two minits six seconds or half a gender rhyme'.

Peter Barnes, Milton Keynes
Notes and Queries, *Guardian*, 15.4.91

★ ★ ★

One morning, about 1933, someone brought into school a copy of the *Bootle Times* which contained a piece about the local find of an ancient Roman pot. Around the rim could faintly be discerned the words ITI SAPIS POTANDA BIGONE. I can't remember when this hoax was first perpetrated but the *Bootle Times* was only one in a long line of victims.

★ ★ ★

The more specialized university disciplines become, the wider the gulf between scholarship and ordinary life, and the harder it is to retain a sense of 'the Idea of a University'. In a recent collection of essays, the distinguished political philosopher Michael Oakeshott offers a lucid summary of what a real university, rather than a training college or a polytechnic, is actually about:

The pursuit of learning is not a race in which the competitors jockey for the best place, it is not even an argument or a symposium; it is a conversation. And the peculiar virtue of a university (as a place of man studies) is to exhibit it in this character, each study appearing as a voice whose tone is neither tyrannous nor plangent, but humble and conversable. A conversation does not need a chairman, it has no predetermined course, we do not ask what it is 'for', and we do not judge its excellence by its conclusion; it has no conclusion, but is always put by for another day. Its integration is not superimposed but springs from the quality of the voices which speak, and its value lies in the relics it leaves behind in the mind of those who participate...

A university will have ceased to exist when its learning has degenerated into what is now called research, when its teaching has become mere instruction and occupies the whole of an undergraduate's time, and when those who came to be taught come, not in search of their intellectual fortune but with a vitality so unroused or so exhausted that they wish only to be provided with a serviceable moral and intellectual outfit; when they come with no understanding of the manners of conversation but desire only a qualification for earning a living or a certificate to let them in on the exploitation of the world.

Review of *The Voice of Liberal Learning: Michael Oakeshott on Education*, edited by Timothy Fuller (Yale University Press, 1989). *Oxford Today*, Hilary Term issue, 1990

★ ★ ★

Oakeshott's idea of a conversation is an appropriate image for the tutorial at its best. Oxford graduates through the ages have testified to its value – both by wryly admitting their failure to benefit from it, and by gracefully thanking their alma mater for an unforgettable experience.

Ibid.

★ ★ ★

'Marcus Tullius Cicero,' I began, 'was born at Arpinum on 3 January BC 106.' 'No, never,' cried my tutor, 'under any circumstances begin an essay like that.' And he started me off on half a dozen different tracks. What did Cicero stand for? Was he a genuine politician? Was he a trimmer? Did he do good for the state or evil? 'Begin with an epigram, begin with a paradox, or begin with a demonstrably false paradox, or begin with a demonstrably false paradox and demolish it. But never, never, start off with such a dry and helpless statement as that Marcus Tullius Cicero was born at Arpinum on 3 January BC 106.'

The whole of Oxford teaching was in that condemnation – ideas, not facts; judgements, not an index; life, not death.

Arthur Waugh, on his tutor Professor Charles Oman, ibid.

★ ★ ★

Never judge a man by his umbrella. It may not be his.

Notice on Eton master's schoolroom, quoted by Quentin Letts, *Daily Telegraph*, 27.10.97

★ ★ ★

There were not many girls at Millfield then. Boss called us the YLD – the Young Ladies' Club. I broke one rule too many and was discovered in the orchard after dark with a boy – sniffed out by the alsatian belonging to Amothe Sankey, Boss's secretary. I was summoned to Boss's study the next morning. In the presence of the inscrutable Miss Sankey he told me that I would be expelled, but the boy would not, because 'it's always the woman's fault'. A harsh doctrine. Because I was sitting the Oxford entrance examination, I was allowed to stay till the end of term, and left under a cloud no bigger than a man's hand. Boss gave me a very red, very sticky, Charles of the Ritz lipstick as a leaving present.

Victoria Glendinning obituary of Jack Meyer, *The Times*, 16.3.91

★ ★ ★

Sir – On the subject of a university education and its doubtful usefulness in the ordinary world, I came across this quotation in *Oxford Remembered* by Harold Macmillan.

'Gentlemen – you are now about to embark upon a course of studies which will occupy you for two years . . . Some of you . . . will go into the Church, or to the Bar, or the House of Commons . . . or into various professions . . . A few – I hope a very few – will become teachers or dons . . . nothing you will learn . . . will be of the slightest possible use to you in after life – save only this: . . . you should be able to detect when a man is talking rot, and that . . . is the main, if not the sole, purpose of education.'

This seems to be a fair definition of education.
Peter Craig, Rochdale, Lancs, letter to *Daily Telegraph*, 10.4.91

# This Land of Heroes(?)
*(England and the English)*

Go into the London Exchange, a place of more dignity than many courts, you will find representatives of all nations assembled there to promote human welfare; there the Jew, the Mohammedan and the Christian deal with one another as though they were of the same religion; the only person whom they count as infidels are those who go bankrupt; there the Presbyterian trusts the Anabaptist and the Anglican accepts the Quaker's promise. When they leave these peaceful and free assemblies, some go to the Synagogue, others go to have a drink, this one goes to have himself baptized in a large cistern in the name of the Father proceeding via the Son to the Holy Ghost; that one has his son's foreskin cut off, mumbling over the child some Hebrew words which he does not understand; those others go to their church with their hats on waiting for divine inspiration, and all are content.

If there were only one religion in English, there would be a risk of despotism, if there were two they would cut each other's throats; as it is, there are thirty, and they live happily in peace.

Voltaire, *Lettres Philosophiques*, VI, 1737

★ ★ ★

As a matter of fact, golf clubs usually know how to deal with difficulties of this sort. Take the Great Braces Affair which occurred a few years ago at a famous Scottish links. On a rare hot August afternoon, one elderly member spied another elderly member playing in shirtsleeves and displaying bright purple-and-gold braces. He protested to the Hon Sec that he could not possibly remain a member of a club which permitted such behaviour, braces were the thin end of the wedge, it would be bathing suits next, and so on. When hauled before the committee, the other elderly member retorted that he would not dream of staying in a club which was so intolerant, this was an infringement of the liberty of the individual and the spirit of Hume and Adam Smith, etc. Impasse. To and fro the battle raged, other members resigned in sympathy, there were threats of a mass boycott of the autumn foursomes.

And then some Solomon of the 19th green – a judge of the Court of Sessions perhaps, a Writer to the Signet at the very least – proposed the solution: that the wearing of braces should be strictly forbidden, except in August and by members of more than twenty years standing. And there the matter, amicably, rests, an example to us all.

Ferdinand Mount, *Daily Telegraph*, 30.11.85

\* \* \*

The Eton College diary is clear in its priorities when giving procedure for pupils in the event of a bomb warning:

Action to be taken by boys on the alarm signal:
1 In the built-up area, take cover inside the nearest building.
2 Inside rooms, open windows and close curtains.
3 On the playing fields, continue games.

Peterborough, *Daily Telegraph*, 24.11.88

\* \* \*

I am grateful to the journal of the National Trust for a couple of anecdotes concerning the Trust's stately-homes guides.

A new guide at Quebec House in Westerham was apparently moved to confess to a colleague, 'I've just given a visitor some completely false information – but I do think it better to be wrong *positively* rather than admit to ignorance.'

Another, at Dudmaston in Shropshire, once rounded on a young man persecuting him with obscure questions. He said: 'Sir, I am not here to educate you, I am here to ensure you do not nick anything.'

Peterborough, *Daily Telegraph*, 7.6.85

★ ★ ★

A leaflet handed to visitors at Southend's Roller City says:

> No chewing gum anywhere; no smoking; no food or drink to be brought in; no studded leather jackets; no torn, worn or scruffy clothing/shoes; no working overalls or hats; no foul language or anti-social behaviour; no bullying or pushing; no loitering or smoking in the toilets; no children under 14 on the balcony; no Doctor Marten boots; no boots with steel toecaps; no dogs; no black tow stops or wheels; no cup and cone bearings; no axles to extend beyond wheels; no floor powder; no worn or dirty street skates. Have a nice day.

Ibid.

★ ★ ★

Julian Critchley, Tory MP, tells of lunching with former prime minister, Harold Macmillan, at Birch Grove. On a table was a copy of *My Life* by Oswald Mosley, which had just been published. I drew his attention to it. 'Ah, Tom Mosley, quite the most able man I have ever met; but quite mad. He came to me once and said, "Harold, I am thinking of putting my people in black shirts." "A mistake," I said, "whenever the British feel strongly about anything they wear tweed jackets and grey flannel trousers."'

Julian Critchley, *Daily Telegraph*, 28.5.84

★ ★ ★

Displayed on a bus shelter in Bristol is a poster which asks: 'Where will *you* be on Judgement Day?' Beneath it someone has written, 'Still here waiting for the next bus to Keynsham.'
London Day by Day, *Daily Telegraph*, 25.7.85

★ ★ ★

The English instinctively admire any man who has no talent and is modest about it.
James Agate

★ ★ ★

An Englishman thinks he is moral when he is only uncomfortable.
G B Shaw

★ ★ ★

Eccentricity exists particularly in the English because of that peculiar and satisfactory knowledge of infallibility that is the hallmark and birthright of the British Nation.
Edith Sitwell

★ ★ ★

With respect to Goethe there was a short obituary notice of him in the *Examiner*...so rare in this country is any, even the most commonplace, knowledge of Germany, that none of the other papers gave any observations at all on the extinction of the greatest man then living in Europe...
John Stuart Mill in a letter to Carlyle, 1852

★ ★ ★

The sun never sets on the British Empire because God wouldn't trust an Englishman in the dark.
Anon

The English think they are free, but they are only so during the election of Members of Parliament. Afterwards they are slaves, they are nothing. During the brief moment of their liberty, the use which they make of it merits well that they should lose it.

Jean-Jacques Rousseau, *Du Contrat Social*, III, 1761

\* \* \*

When Kingslake, the explorer, encountered a fellow Englishman crossing the Sinai Desert in 1835, he commented: 'We passed each other quite as distantly as if we had passed in Pall Mall.'

*Evening Standard*, 5.1.83

\* \* \*

An Englishman's mind works best when it is almost too late.

Lord D'Abernon

\* \* \*

The British people, being subject to fogs and possessing a powerful middle class, require grave statesmen.

Disraeli, quoted by Ferdinand Mount, *Daily Telegraph*, 9.11.85

\* \* \*

English society in the mid-eighteenth century, according to Daniel Defoe, was divided into seven categories.

1. The great, who live profusely,
2. The rich, who live plentifully,
3. The middle sort, who live well,
4. The working traders, who labour hard but feel no want,
5. The country people, farmers etc., who fare indifferently,

6. The poor, who fare hard,
7. The miserable, that really pinch and suffer want.

Quoted in *Rococo* (Victoria & Albert Museum), 1984, page 12

★ ★ ★

When will it be grasped that almost everyone who has employed anyone will do almost anything to avoid repeating the experience.

Letter to the *Financial Times* from Roger Pemlington, (managing director, Heathrow Business Centre), 1.8.95 (unemployment at 3,100,000)

★ ★ ★

When Mr Bob Payton, the Chicago-born fast food millionaire, says that queuing is a great national pastime in Britain, he probably intends it as some sort of sneer. The implication is that we are a slavish lot, lacking in individualism and initiative and suffering from an excess of stoicism.

Mr Payton makes this remark in *The Chicagoan's Guide to London*. I am not bothered about his strictures on things like the telephone system and the standard of pubs, but describing queuing as a 'pastime' is like calling the Taj Mahal a building. It is far more than that; it is a work of art. Still, Mr Payton has lived here for only fourteen years, which is scarcely time enough to get to the front of the queue at the box office of the National Theatre, let alone to understand the finer points of life in this country.

I was lucky enough to participate in an excellent forty-minute queue at the taxi rank at Victoria Station the other day, but the performance was nearly spoiled for me by the presence of foreign tourists — many, no doubt, from Chicago — who did not fully understand the ritual. They did not appreciate the more subtle movements and passages, particularly that magical moment of hope when, as if by telepathy, all the people in the queue pick up their suitcases and shuffle forward three paces in unison. The telepathic aspect is present in all the highest quality queues. I have seen a line of people transformed into a thirty-yard embodiment of silent moral outrage as one single person has broken the rules of etiquette and, for example, saved a place for a friend.

A truly classic queue is like a line of infantrymen at Waterloo (the battle, not the station), holding firm, disciplined and unflinching, as the enemy pours towards it. You used to see this in the old-fashioned bus queues as the Number 45 crept ever nearer through the traffic. With pay-as-you-enter buses all that has degenerated into a genteel jostle.

Oliver Pritchett, *Daily Telegraph*, 28.7.87

\* \* \*

Baron Philippe de Rothschild loved jokes. In the château at Mouton is a large rug depicting Queen Victoria and Napoleon III, woven to celebrate the Anglo-French commercial treaty of 1860.

He would say to an English guest, 'We can never decide whether the figures are life-size or larger. Would you be kind enough to lie down and measure yourself against one of them?'

The man would comply – but to his host's glee would invariably lie on top of the emperor, rather than on Queen Victoria.

Albany (Kenneth Rose), *Sunday Telegraph*, 24.1.88, page 10

\* \* \*

Whatever the world thinks of the English they give us points for three things: the lushness of our grass, the mettle of our horses and the beauty of our children. Yet when all three are brought together, we, who speak Shakespeare's tongue, call the occasion a gymkhana.

MacDonald Hastings, journalist and broadcaster, obituary, *The Times*, 6.10.82

\* \* \*

In England there are sixty different religions and only one sauce.

Francesco Caraccioli (eighteenth-century gourmet)

★ ★ ★

I wasted several years of my life in the supposition that England was a great nation.

Bismark

★ ★ ★

20 November 1777 – William Pitt, Earl of Chatham, addresses the House of Lords on the revolt of the American colonies: 'This ruinous and ignominious situation, where we cannot act with success, nor suffer with honour, calls upon us to remonstrate in the strongest and loudest language of truth, to rescue the ear of Majesty from the delusions which surround it. I love and honour the English troops; I know their virtues and their valour; I know they can achieve anything except impossibilities; and I know the conquest of English America is an impossibility. You cannot conquer America. If I were an American, as I am an Englishman, while a foreign troop was landed in my country, I would never lay down my arms. Never, never, never.'

★ ★ ★

Michael Howard, the Minister for Water and Planning, told this story at the annual lunch given by Euram, the headhunters, yesterday. A new British ambassador to the US was asked by the *Washington Post* what he wanted for Christmas and the New Year. 'In no way can I accept a gift from the *Washington Post*,' he insisted. A few hours later his secretary told him the paper was on the telephone again. 'Well, I suppose a small box of crystallized fruits would be just about acceptable,' he said.

The next day he read in the *Washington Post*: 'The Soviet ambassador wants further progress on general disarmament for Christmas and the New Year. The French ambassador wants peace in the Middle East. The British ambassador wants a small box of crystallized fruits.'

★ ★ ★

Asked at a conference of Americans in Hawaii to define the essence of an English club, Nick Cranfield who runs the RAC in Pall Mall said: 'It is that we would prefer a silver salt cellar that doesn't work to a plastic one that does.'
Peterborough, *Daily Telegraph*, 5.11.93

★ ★ ★

The English do not care much for music, but they do like the noise it makes.
Sir Thomas Beecham, 1961

# Shadowlands
*(Films)*

True stories are hardest to write. When your script uses exactly what the real characters said, it lacks the ring of truth. It's dull.
Carl Foreman (film director and scriptwriter) to Vicky Elliot, *New York Herald Tribune*, 13.8.82

\* \* \*

Strip the phoney tinsel off Hollywood and you'll only find the real tinsel underneath.
Oscar Levant

\* \* \*

I prefer films to newspapers because papers tell lies about real people and films tell the truth about imaginary ones.
G K Chesterton

\* \* \*

To justify a sequel you have to have a successful film and one in which the third act is not literally the final act. I don't know how you could do a sequel to *Hamlet*.
Robert Chartoff (co-producer of *Rocky, Rocky II* and *Rocky III*), *Sunday Telegraph*, 8.8.82

\* \* \*

George Bernard Shaw was once offered a job writing scripts

for Sam Goldwyn. Explaining his refusal, Shaw said, 'The trouble, Mr Goldwyn, is that you are only interested in art – and I am only interested in money.'

* * *

Harry Cohn was a much loathed Hollywood tycoon. Seeing the crowd at his funeral, the comedian Red Skelton said: 'It proves what they always say: give the public what it wants to see, and they'll always come out for it.'

* * *

*The Lavender Hill Mob*, starring Alec Guinness (1951), concerned a minor, crushed bank clerk who organizes the robbery of the Bank of England. While preparing his script, T E B Clarke made enquiries of the bank itself, where he was required to fill out a form headed 'Nature of Business'. He duly wrote, 'How to rob the bank of a million pounds.' The bank could not have been more helpful: 'The way we robbed the bank was precisely the way suggested by its officials,' said Clarke.

Obituary of T E B Clarke, *Daily Telegraph*, 13.2.89

* * *

*Double Indemnity*, the critics said, was a good picture that was the beginning of the classic *film noir*. I don't know what these critics mean by '*film noir*'. I don't know nothing.

Billy Wilder at eighty-seven in interview with Stephen M Silverman, *The Times*, 10.7.93

* * *

The Russian film *Hands* is one of the most disturbing films you will ever see – if, that is, you want to see it. Its heroes are

Dostoevsky's Insulted And Injured: a man who moves around in a broken bathtub, a woman who has lain on the ground for forty years, a rag collector building a pile of rubbish to reach the sky, a dumb boy who has escaped from an asylum to live in a hovel in the ground, an old hunchback who keeps the head of her executioner in a wooden box, a blind beggar family who work the streets of Kishinev. Collectively, they make for one of the most miserable nights out at the cinema you're likely to get.

Their histories and sorrows unfold on screen with inexorable slowness. The viewer will either be sucked in as a witness to their terrible lives or turn away, unable to take so much misery. The film has won its director, Artur Aristakisyan, prizes in Moscow, Berlin, Taormina, San Francisco, Karlovy Vary and Munich.

Isobel Montgomery, *Guardian*, 28.8.98

# Feet Under the Table

*(Food and Wine)*

Outside every fat man there is an even fatter man trying to close in.

Kingsley Amis, *One Fat Englishman*

★ ★ ★

On seeing Stafford Cripps's vegetarian dinner, Winston Churchill remarked: 'Are you about to eat that or have you just finished?'

*Spectator*, 2.7.82, page 21

★ ★ ★

Is there not something deeply corrupt and decadent in eating very expensive food specifically designed to keep you slim? After all, the idea of a retributory coronary striking dead the self-indulgent patrician helps to persuade the poor that there is some justice in the world, and a culinary system which mitigates the sanction is therefore anti-social.

Paul Johnson, *Daily Telegraph*, 29.10.83

★ ★ ★

The most memorable wine drinking session of my life was a staff banquet at Buckingham Palace. I was an ADC-General to the Queen. It was a splendid occasion, with over a hundred guests, gold plate for the hot dishes and Sèvres setting for the rest. The service was from men in the royal livery, each with only a few guests to look after. 'Sherry, Sir John?' said a velvety voice over my right shoulder, as the soup came up in its gold plate. 'Thank you: I'd like some sherry.' Then Balmoral salmon and the velvet voice again. 'Hock, Sir John?' 'Thank you. I have been looking forward to this Johannisberger.' 'It will not disappoint you, Sir John.' Something else to eat. 'Claret, Sir John?' 'Thank you: it is good to meet this Margaux.' 'You will find it a noble wine, Sir John.' The ice pudding arrived. 'Château Yquem, Sir John, or champagne?' 'I have a difficulty here. I should love the Yquem but what I really think I need is a glass of champagne.' 'Then may I make a suggestion, Sir John, that I give you both?' Excellent man. I never at any time saw his face but the trust between us was complete.

General Sir John Hackett, *Vogue*, January 1983

\* \* \*

Randolph Churchill was annoyed about the quality of a dinner he had with his American cousins, the Vanderbilts. 'Imagine,' he complained, 'they served mayonnaise out of a bottle. Even worse they had lobster as the main course. I told them in no uncertain terms that only jumped-up people served lobster as a main course.'

Told to Milton Shulman by Randolph Churchill

\* \* \*

I have always found it remarkable that in poetic and romantic literature there is so much about sex and very little about food which is just as pleasurable and never lets you down.

W H Auden

\* \* \*

Dame Edith Evans, grand old lady of the English stage, shopping for groceries at London's most exclusive shop,

Fortnum and Mason's, received a bill for £4 19s 5d. She was shocked at the total amount. '£4 19s 5d seems a somewhat exorbitant sum to pay for a loaf of bread, a packet of tea and a jar of fish paste,' she thundered to the young tail-coated salesman, imperiously handing him a five pound note. 'You may keep the change. I believe I trod on a grape when I entered the shop.'

Sue Arnold, *Observer Magazine*, 19.9.82

\* \* \*

Michael Meyer, translator of Ibsen, was at the cashier's desk of the Savile Club one lunch hour when he heard Sir Ralph Richardson, waiting behind him to pay his bill, asking aloud of anyone within earshot, 'There's nothing particularly odd about a jam omelette, is there?' Meyer asked him what the matter was. Richardson replied: 'I ordered a jam omelette from the waitress and she told me, "Sir, we have all kinds of omelettes, ham, tomato, cheese but I don't know if there's a jam omelette." So I said to her, "Well you know, a jam omelette's not all that difficult, once you have the general idea of an omelette." And so in the end she said, "I'll go and ask the cook." So off she went and came back and said, "Cook wanted to know who it was for – what name am I to give?" I gave my name and off she went; a second time she returned: "I'm very sorry, sir, cook says they can't do it for you." At this point Richardson turned to Meyer and said, 'What I want to know is, who do you have to be in this club in order to get a jam omelette?'

From *Ralph Richardson* by Larry O'Connor, page 188

\* \* \*

Ann Leslie, *Daily Mail* journalist, at a Royal Garden Party in the hot summer of 1983, was queuing up for some cold lemonade along with a clutch of bishops. The fierce waitress

Sir Ralph Richardson

behind the table told the thirsty guests that the glasses had run out and they would have to wait until some more arrived. Miss Leslie, very hot and impatient with the delay, suggested that she wouldn't mind having lemonade out of one of the cups on the table. 'The cups are for tea and not lemonade,' said the waitress, firmly. As Ann began to remonstrate, she was admonished by the Suffragan Bishop of Taunton standing beside her. 'There are some places where iced lemonade can be served in a cup,' he said, 'but a Royal Garden Party is not one of them.'

*Stop the Week*, BBC Radio 4, 2.7.83

\* \* \*

Harry Yoxall, Condé Nast publisher, who has died in his eighty-eighth year, was an imaginative gourmet. When King George V died in 1936 Yoxall gave this dinner to his friends:

> Caviare with vodka (for white is also a mourning colour);
> Octopus in its own black ink;
> Black pudding with a very dark Cahors *Noir*;
> Prunes *flambées* in Mirabelle.

The old king would surely have approved.

Kenneth Rose, *Sunday Telegraph*, Spring 1984

\* \* \*

The French ambassador and his wife, Bobby and Hélène de Margerie, were planning an ambrosial dinner and their chef in London showed them his proposed menu. 'What is Velouté de Nymphes?' asked the ambassador. 'A fragrant cream soup made from frogs' legs.' 'Not for our British friends,' said the ambassador, 'they would dislike the idea of eating frogs.' 'They would never know, your excellency.' 'Oh, but we could not deceive our guests, could we?'

Kenneth Rose, *Sunday Telegraph*, 23.11.84

\* \* \*

## HENRY KING

### *Who chewed bits of string, and was early cut off in dreadful agony*

The chief defect of Henry King
Was chewing little bits of string.
At last he swallowed some which tied
Itself in ugly knots inside.
Physicians of the Utmost Fame,
were called at once; but when they came
They answered as they took their fees,
'There is no cure for this disease
Henry will very soon be dead.'
His parents stood about his bed,
Lamenting his untimely death,
When Henry, with his latest breath,
Cried – 'Oh, my friends, be warned by me,
That breakfast, dinner, lunch and tea,
Are all the human frame requires . . .'
With that the wretched child expires.

Hilaire Belloc, *Cautionary Tales*, 1907

★ ★ ★

When I first went to Canada someone told me of a recent immigrant from Hungary who knew the English words for only one meal. Every day for three weeks he went into the local diner and gave his order: 'Spaghetti, apple pie.' Then, up to here with spaghetti and apple pie, a friend taught him another combination.

Next day he gave his new order: 'Toasted cheese, waffle.' 'Canadian, English, Scotch, Irish?' the waitress asked. 'White, rye, pumpernickel, granary, wholewheat? Pickle, gherkin, mayonnaise, mustard, lettuce, tomato, bacon? Ice cream, honey, syrup, molasses? Huh? *Huh?*' The poor guy shrugged, defeated. 'Spaghetti, apple pie,' he said.

Jill Tweedie, *Guardian*, 19.8.86

Spike Milligan, who was staying at the Shelbourne Hotel in Dublin, ordered supper with two bottles of wine to be served to him in his room when he got back from the TV studio of Telefis Eireann. But the waiter, when he finally arrived with his trolley, brought in two dinners and four bottles of wine. 'Oh, Jasus, I tought there was two of you,' said the waiter apologetically. 'What'll I do with the second dinner? Shall I take it away, or will you eat it or shall I leave it here?' Milligan asked the waiter if he had eaten and when he said no, invited the man to join him. 'I'll eat it for you, sor,' said the waiter, sitting down and polishing off the dinner along with three of the four bottles of wine. 'By the way,' he concluded, 'can I be perfectly truthful with you sor? I'd have thought a man with your money could have afforded a better bloody dinner than this.'

Richard Ingrams, *Independent*, 15.4.88

\* \* \*

Hélène, a French cook for Gertrude Stein, did not like Matisse. She said a Frenchman should not stay unexpectedly to a meal, particularly if he asked the servant beforehand what there was for dinner. She said foreigners had a perfect right to do these things but not a Frenchman, and Matisse had once done it. So when Miss Stein said to her, 'Monsieur Matisse is staying for dinner this evening,' she would say, 'in that case I will not make an omelette but fry the eggs. It takes the same number of eggs and the same amount of butter but it shows less respect and he will understand.'

Elizabeth David, *Mediterranean Food*, page 31

\* \* \*

At a luncheon Baron Philippe de Rothschild gave, to celebrate the upgrading of his Mouton Rothschild to its rightful place among the first growths of the original 1855 classification, he invited his near-neighbours and cousins who grow the equally lustrous Château Lafite.

As one of his cousins lifted a glass of Mouton to his lips, he said: 'Tell me, Philippe, it is several years since I was last here. Where exactly does your property begin?' 'On the other side of that wall, about fifty metres away.' 'What a pity your beautiful wine does not travel.'

Albany (Kenneth Rose), *Sunday Telegraph*, 24.1.88

\* \* \*

Disraeli was at a ghastly dinner and each of the six courses was worse than the preceding one. The butler then announced that there would be champagne. 'At last,' cried Disraeli, 'thank God for something warm.'

\* \* \*

A customer in a seedy Chicago café called the waitress after sniffing the food she had served him. 'Do you know what the cook did to this fish?' he asked. 'Sure,' said the waitress, 'she grilled it.' 'So now you should take it back to her,' said the customer. 'It's ready to talk.'

\* \* \*

The Anglo-Saxon view of a banquet can be expressed in terms of the history of the world. You begin with soup – water with things swimming in it – then move on to the aqueous kingdom, then to flying creatures, then to mammals. Finally you celebrate man in cheeses and desserts, both products of sophisticated culture.

Anthony Burgess, *The Times*, 7.8.82

\* \* \*

I was with an Australian couple just back from Europe. The wife opened a can of Heinz spaghetti saying 'Nice to get back to something genuine after all that foreign stuff.'

Anthony Burgess, *The Times*, 7.8.82

\* \* \*

Why is it that every place but here, the cauliflower is a very nice vegetable?
Lewis Carroll

★ ★ ★

My heart is Catholic, but my stomach is Lutheran.
Erasmus, explaining his dislike of fish

★ ★ ★

In England eating out seems to have taken the place of church. The congregation climbs into its Sunday best to be ushered into its pews by sanctimonious head waiters. Once seated they talk in awestruck whispers, look furtively round at other worshippers and would no more think of complaining about the two minute slices of duck's breast, simmering in black-currant juice and decorated with a bit of raw broccoli and a kiwi fruit, than they would of interrupting the sermon. Some of the worst offenders are restaurants opened in English country houses where you are often made to feel that you have trespassed on the privacy of a solemn weekend gathering and there has just been a death in the family.
John Mortimer, *Daily Telegraph*, 25.7.87

★ ★ ★

Lord Leconfield, owner of Petworth, loved bananas. Dining at Petworth, a guest told him that nobody really knew how good a banana could be unless he tasted one straight off the tree. Next day Leconfield sent his head gardener off to Kew to learn how to grow them. A special greenhouse was built, a banana tree planted. At length a single fruit appeared and was allowed to ripen. It was placed before Leconfield at the end of dinner one night. He peeled it with a golden knife, cut a slice, place it in his mouth with a golden fork. 'Oh, God,' he shouted. 'It tastes like any other damn banana!' It had cost him three thousand pounds and he never grew another.

Kenneth Rose, told to him by Lord Egremont, grandson of Lord
Leconfield, *Sunday Telegraph*, 27.3.85

* * *

Breakfast – the noble dish of egg and bacon – should be eaten
four times a day when one is in England.

W Somerset Maugham, quoted in *English Companion* by Godfrey Smith,
page 43

* * *

During these three nightmare years we talked about wine
practically every day. It was our last link with the world of the
living. Hungry, cold, hot, fearful, we never stopped talking about
wine. About claret to begin with, but we were not choosy. Many
of our fictional pilgrimages took place in Champagne. And how
should you open a bottle of champagne? By grasping the cork
delicately in the hand or shooting it right across the room? Such
were the subjects of our discussions while all the time there was
death in our souls.

During the three months after my liberation, I did not drink
any claret. I had made a vow. One day in 1987 I was left for twelve
hours in one of the iron coffins which our kidnappers used for
the clandestine transfer of prisoners. That day I thought I was
going to die. I believed that my warders had abandoned me in a
disused quarry where I heard only the sound of drops of water
dripping in the silence. I was trembling with cold and sheer
terror. So I prayed to the Lord: if I get out alive from this
nightmare I'll never touch another drop of alcohol. But then I
thought better of it: was life worth living without claret? So I
compromised on three months, proof that even in this moment
of extreme privation, my soul was not totally desolate.

Jean-Paul Kauffman, from *L'Amateur de Bordeaux*, *Financial Times*, 24.9.88.
Kauffman was kidnapped in Lebanon in May 1985 and held hostage till
released on 4 May 1988

* * *

When the supply of barley ran short during the Second World War, Churchill issued a defiant decree: 'On no account reduce the barley for whisky: it would be improvident not to preserve this characteristic British element of ascendancy.'

Leader, *The Times*, 28.5.94

\* \* \*

Ever since I commented elsewhere in this newspaper about our increasingly nervous attitude towards food, people have been asking me whether this era of homogenized, sanitized, sealed food has impaired our digestive capacities. The best answer I can give them is to offer this account of Lord Palmerston's appetite in his eighty-first year. In about 1864, the Speaker of the House of Commons had dinner with Palmerston and left this account.

> 'He ate for dinner two plates of turtle soup; he was then served very amply to a plate of cod and oyster sauce; he then took a pâté, afterwards he was helped to two very greasy-looking entrées; he then dispatched a plate of roast mutton; there then appeared before him the largest, and to my mind the hardest, slice of ham that ever figured on the table of a nobleman; yet it disappeared, just in time to answer the inquiry of his butler: 'Snipe or pheasant, my lord?' He instantly replied: 'Pheasant.' Thus he completed his ninth dish of meat at the meal.'

From which I judge that our digestions are *not* what they were.

W F Deedes, *Daily Telegraph*, 31.7.89

\* \* \*

The customer profile of Marks and Spencer's food stores is not as up-market as is sometimes supposed, it seems. Sales of vichyssoise doubled when it was renamed leek-and-potato soup.

Diary, *Financial Times*, 15.6.92

\* \* \*

When the playwright Arthur Miller took Marilyn Monroe to have dinner with his parents, she was offered, by his Orthodox Jewish father, a second bowl of matzo-ball soup, which she finished. When Marilyn declined another refill, Isadore, his father, became alarmed. 'You don't like our matzo-ball soup?' he asked. 'Gee, I love it,' said Marilyn, 'but isn't there any other part of a matzo you can eat?'

From *Marilyn Monroe* by Barbara Leaming, 1998

\* \* \*

The French ambassador in Washington, soon after the great Wall Street Crash, said: 'Between the crisis and the catastrophe, there is always time for a glass of champagne.'

# So You Don't Like the Other Joke

### *(Goldberg and Jewish Jokes)*

Goldberg and Cohen were on Safari in Africa. A lion leapt through the opening of their tent and then dashed out again. 'What was that?' asked the terrified Cohen. 'How should I know? I'm not a furrier,' said Goldberg.

★ ★ ★

Cohen and Goldberg were walking in a garden and Cohen pointed to a daisy. 'What kind of a flower is that? he asked Goldberg. 'How should I know?' replied Goldberg, 'I'm not an embroiderer.'

★ ★ ★

Goldberg and Cohen are facing a Nazi firing squad. Just as the firing squad raises its rifles to despatch them, Cohen holds up his hand. 'Please, Herr Lieutenant,' he calls to the officer in charge of the squad, 'can I have a blindfold, please?' Goldberg nudges him and whispers, 'Cohen, don't make trouble.'

★ ★ ★

Goldberg met Mrs Cohen in the Bronx a few days after her husband's funeral. 'What a fine and tasteful funeral you gave your husband,' said Goldberg.

'Oh, I'm so glad you liked it,' said Mrs Cohen.

'Everything was just perfect,' said Goldberg.

'Did you notice where the grave was?' said Mrs Cohen, 'On

a hill with a superb view. And that casket! Did you know it was made from the finest oak? And the handles were genuine gold-plated. The name-plate was made of real gold.'

'Mm-hm,' said Goldberg, shaking his head appreciatively, 'it must have cost you a lot of money.'

'A lot of money! It cost eighteen thousand dollars!'

'Eighteen thousand dollars!' exclaimed Goldberg. 'My goodness, for another five thousand dollars you could have buried him in a Cadillac.'

★ ★ ★

On seeing Mrs Goldberg's granddaughter seated in the back seat of a Cadillac, Mrs Cohen says: 'What a beautiful grand-daughter you have, Mrs Goldberg. How old is she?' 'Well, she's nearly three.' 'Does she walk yet?' 'No, thank God, she doesn't have to.'

★ ★ ★

A cockney Jewish taxi-driver emigrated to America where he took up his trade in New York. Seen by a friend a few years later, he was asked what he thought about New York. 'It's a nice place to live. I only have two things against it – one is the racial prejudice and the other is the schwarzers.'

★ ★ ★

At Mrs Goldberg's front door, a tramp asks her if she can spare him any food. 'I haven't eaten for two days and I'm starving.' 'Do you mind eating yesterday's food?' asks Mrs Goldberg. 'No, not at all. I'm very hungry.' 'All right then,' says Mrs Goldberg, 'come tomorrow.'

★ ★ ★

The three wise men groped their way in the dark to the Bethlehem manger. In the background they could faintly see Joseph and a small crib. One of the trio accidentally stepped on a rake which came up and hit him on the forehead. 'Jesus Christ!' he exclaimed in pain.

'That's a very good name,' said Joseph. 'Jesus. We were going to call him Maurice.'

Jack Lee (Milton Shulman and Ned Sherrin's barber)

* * *

Why do Jewish husbands die before their wives? Because they want to.

* * *

A Jewish son received a telegram from his mother. It read: 'Letter following. Start worrying.'

* * *

Cohen meets his old friend, Goldberg, after many years and asks him what business he's in now.

'I'm in the building trade,' replies Goldberg.

'A very good business,' says Cohen. 'And what then are you building?'

'I'm building a cathedral.'

'A cathedral. How interesting! It must take a long time and be very expensive,' says Cohen.

'A long time! I've been on it for eight years. And expensive? Don't ask. I've had to import special wood from the Lebanon for the pews, the glass for the stained glass windows comes from Venice. And I've got six artists fulltime painting angels and cherubs and saints on the ceiling. It's costing me a fortune.'

'Ah,' says Cohen, 'and who are you building it for?'

'Who am I building it for? I'm building it on spec.'

* * *

Goldberg was showing Cohen around his grocery store. In the cellar, Goldberg pointed out huge crates of cheese. 'Here we have the finest Stilton, next to them is the Cheddar and over there is a new arrival of Gorgonzola,' said Goldberg, waving his hand at the packed boxes of cheese.

'My goodness,' said Cohen, 'you must sell a lot of cheese in your shop.'

'Me?' replied Goldberg. 'Me sell cheese? I can't sell cheese but the man who sells me cheese, can he sell cheese!'

★ ★ ★

On passing his lawyer in the street, Goldberg calls out, 'Nice day, isn't it.' On reflection, he turns back, catches up his lawyer and says, 'I'm telling you, not asking you.'

★ ★ ★

In Piccadilly, Mr Goldberg met the rabbi of his synagogue. 'Mr Goldberg,' said the rabbi in the course of the conversation, 'I've always admired the way you look just like an Englishman. Such elegance! I've always wanted to look like an Englishman. How have you managed to do it?'

'Well,' said Goldberg, 'it's very easy. All you have to do is buy the right clothes. With the right clothes anyone can look like an Englishman.'

'How do you do that? What clothes? Tell me, Goldberg what should I do?'

'Dressing like an Englishman just means going to the right shops. They have the clothes and you just buy them. Now first of all, of course, you have to shave off your long beard and stop wearing that large black hat and those black suits. And take down on a piece of paper these places. For shoes you go to Lobbs. For hats you go to Lock's. For shirts, Turnbull and Asser. For suits, Kilgour and French. For ties and socks, Washington Tremletts. For cuff-links, wallets etc., you go to Asprey's.'

The rabbi duly noted down the names of these shops and thanked Goldberg for his help.

Six months later Goldberg saw the rabbi again in Berkeley Square. 'Rabbi,' said Goldberg, surveying this figure in a beautifully cut tweed suit, sporting a jaunty trilby and carrying a furled umbrella, 'rabbi, I hardly recognized you – you look just like an Englishman.'

'Thank you, Goldberg. I owe it all to you. I carried out your instructions and I'm very grateful for your help.'

'But, rabbi,' said Goldberg. 'You look so unhappy. Do I note a tear in your eye? Why are you crying, rabbi?'

'I'm crying because we lost India,' replied the rabbi.

★ ★ ★

When Goldberg was asked what was two and two, he said, 'Are you buying or selling?'

★ ★ ★

The only thing two Jews ever agree about is how much a third Jew should give to charity.

★ ★ ★

At a Jewish restaurant Goldberg asked a passing waiter what time it was. 'You're not my table!' snapped the waiter.

★ ★ ★

On seeing the prospective bride that the matchmaker had produced for him, young Goldberg was appalled. 'You told me she had the appearance, the bearing, the grace of a queen,' he protested. 'But look at her! She's pimply, cross-eyed and hook-nosed. She slobbers her food, she limps and she's hunchbacked.'

'No need to whisper,' says the matchmaker, 'she's deaf too.'
Mary Kenny, *Daily Telegraph*, 5.5.84

★ ★ ★

On a signpost to Golders Green reading 'Two Miles' a Jewish wag had written underneath: 'To you, a mile-and-a-half.'

\* \* \*

Goldberg went to a doctor for treatment for his loss of memory. 'I can't remember what happened to me last month,' he said. 'I can't remember anything about last week. I can't even remember what happened to me yesterday. What should I do, doctor?'

'Pay now!' replied the doctor.

\* \* \*

Jewish maxim: 'It's better never to have been born. But how many are so lucky?'

\* \* \*

Goldberg was talking to a friend about the unsatisfactory meal he had just had in an expensive restaurant. 'You could hardly eat it. It was really terrible. And such small portions!'

\* \* \*

Elderly Jew hit by car lies dying in the street. A Catholic priest bends over him and asks, 'My man, do you believe in the Father, the Son and the Holy Ghost?' 'Look when I'm dying he's asking me riddles,' the Jew replies.

\* \* \*

Goldberg told his doctor that he was having difficulty with his sex life, which was not as frequent or satisfactory as it once was.

'What you need is some regular exercise,' advised the doctor. 'For the next seven days I want you to run ten miles a day. Ten miles – no more, no less – for seven days. That should cure your problem.'

A week later Goldberg telephoned the doctor to report on the treatment.

'Has it helped?' asked the doctor. 'How is your sex life now?'

'How should I know?' replied Goldberg, 'I'm seventy miles from home.'

\* \* \*

Mrs Goldberg took her grandson, Irving, aged five, to the seaside and suddenly a huge wave picked up Irving and carried him out to sea. Mrs Goldberg, distraught, got down on her knees and prayed to God for his return. 'Please, Lord, save my grandson, Irving. He is my daughter's treasure. It will kill her if he is lost. Take me instead, I'm old. Please bring back our Irving.'

A large wave deposited Irving, alive, at the old lady's feet. She looked down at the boy, wet but unhurt, then looked up at the sky and said, 'He had a hat!'

\* \* \*

Goldberg, at a roulette table in Las Vegas, is approached by a luscious blonde who whispers in his ear: 'I'll do anything you want for three hundred dollars...just anything you want for three hundred dollars.'

There is a long pause while Goldberg assesses the offer. 'All right,' he says, 'paint my house.'

\* \* \*

Mrs Goldberg gave her son two ties for his birthday. When he arrived a week later for dinner, wearing one of the ties, she looked at him accusingly and said, 'So what's wrong with the other tie?'

\* \* \*

114

When Mrs Goldberg lay on her deathbed, she asked her husband about her funeral arrangements. 'Everything is in the best of taste,' Goldberg reassured her. 'There will be four limousines – Rolls-Royces – following the hearse. I will be in the front limousine with the children. Your mother will be in the second limousine. Your brother and your three sisters will be in the third limousine. And your cousins will be in the last car.'

'But, Bernard, why is my mother alone in one limousine?' asked Mrs Goldberg. 'It is an unnecessary expense and anyway I would like it she should be in the front limousine with you and the children. I know you cannot stand the sight of my mother and that you have not been speaking for over a year. But on this occasion, as my last dying wish, can you please make a gesture. Have her sit in the front limousine.'

'All right, Hannah,' said Goldberg, after a long pause. 'You'll have your wish. She'll ride with us. *But it'll spoil my day.*'

★ ★ ★

Goldberg arrived home with the bad news that his doctor had told him he had only eight more hours to live. To make his last hours pleasurable, he asked his wife, Hannah, to make love to him. Two hours later, he asked her to make love again. And two hours later, he asked Hannah for a repeat performance. But when Goldberg, still unsatiated, asked for another, and fourth, session, Hannah protested. 'I'm too tired,' she said. 'It's all right for you. After all, you don't have to get up in the morning.'

★ ★ ★

We ended our meal with the latest joke from Moscow: A Jew goes into an employment bureau but is told there are no jobs for him. 'Why?' he asks.

'I'm glad you asked that,' says the man behind the desk. 'Under *glasnost* we are open and above board about our hiring practices. We don't hire Jews.'

115

'What about the return to the principles of Lenin?' asks the amazed applicant. 'What about strict socialist legality, the Soviet constitution, and the rights of minorities and small nations?'

'And especially,' says the bureaucrat, 'we don't hire stupid Jews.'

Barbara Amiel, *The Times*, 24.5.88

\* \* \*

At a buffet party Mrs Cohen congratulated her hostess, Mrs Goldberg, on the quality of her cookies. 'They are so delicious,' gushed Mrs Cohen, 'I've already had three or four.' 'You've had eight,' replied Mrs Goldberg, 'but who counts?'

\* \* \*

In Brooklyn there was a famous Yiddish theatre where the actors from time to time would be heckled by the audience. In a particularly melodramatic deathbed scene, a doctor is trying to console the sobbing wife of Goldberg, who is supposed to be dying. 'I'm sorry, Mrs Goldberg,' says the stage doctor, 'but there is nothing more to be done for your husband. His life is now in God's hands. There is nothing more that medical science or doctors can do for him.'

From the gallery, a voice calls out, 'Vy don't you give him an enema?'

The doctor steps forward to the front of the stage and shouts back: 'It vouldn't help!'

The gallery voice comes back, 'Vell, it vouldn't hoit!'

\* \* \*

At the end of a meal in an expensive restaurant Cohen and Goldberg are given finger bowls by the waiter.

'What are those for?' whispers Cohen to Goldberg.

'Don't know. Ask the waiter,' says Goldberg.

Cohen beckons the waiter and asks, 'Tell me, please, what are these little plates with water for?'

'They're to put your fingers in,' says the waiter.

'You see,' says Goldberg, 'ask a silly question and you get a silly answer.'

\* \* \*

A *mohel* after fifty years in the circumcision business was given a wallet by his friends made up of foreskins he had cut off during the years.

'Why such a small thing after fifty years of effort?' asked a friend of Goldberg who had organised the gift.

'Ah, you see,' said Goldberg. 'When you stroke it, it becomes a suitcase.'

\* \* \*

When Goldberg went to a psychoanalyst for treatment, he was told by the analyst to lie on the couch and talk only if he felt like it. After an hour's session in which Goldberg didn't open his mouth, the analyst dismissed him and said, 'Seventy-five pounds, please.'

Two weeks later Goldberg came for his second session and was again told to lie on the couch but only to speak if he wanted to and if he had anything to say. Goldberg said nothing and once again at the end of the session the analyst, shaking his hand, said, 'Seventy-five pounds, please.'

At the third session Goldberg went through the same procedure, lying on the couch and saying nothing. But just before he rose from the couch, Goldberg said he finally did have something to say. 'Good,' said the analyst, 'what is it?'

'Do you need a partner?' said Goldberg.

\* \* \*

When Mrs Goldberg went to the offices of *The Times* to place an announcement of her husband's death, it consisted only of two words: 'Goldberg dead.' She was told by the clerk in charge that there was a minimum fee of ten pounds for five words and didn't she want to use up her allowance by adding another three words to her announcement? She returned with five words which read, 'Goldberg dead. Volvo for sale.'

★ ★ ★

A Jewish doctor gave Goldberg six months to live. Goldberg couldn't pay his bills so the doctor gave him another six months.

Bernard Manning, *Independent*, 28.4.95

★ ★ ★

Goldberg went to a psychiatrist who told him he was crazy. 'I want a second opinion,' said Goldberg. 'OK,' said the psychiatrist, 'you're ugly, too.'

Henry Youngman (died February 1998 aged ninety-one), quoted by Simon Heffer, *Guardian*, 28.2.98

# No One Lives Forever

*(Health, Medicine and Doctors)*

During a black molasses health fad, Groucho Marx said, 'Black molasses doesn't make you live longer. It just seems longer.'

\* \* \*

> The very fact that I'm relaxed,
> To worry quite impervious,
> When everybody else is taut,
> It's just what makes me nervous.

Anon

\* \* \*

A doctor tells a heart transplant patient that he can offer him three hearts. One from an athlete, one from a young housewife and one from a sixty-five-year-old international banker. Which would he like?

'That of the sixty-five-year-old banker, please,' said the patient.

'Why?' asked the surprised doctor.

'Because I know it has never been used,' said the patient.

\* \* \*

An American surgeon lecturing medical students in Bristol was asked if he considered the operation he was describing was a valuable one. 'Valuable?' demanded the surgeon, a little taken aback. 'I raised five kids on it.'

\* \* \*

Six hours sleep for a man, seven for a woman and eight for a fool.

English proverb

★ ★ ★

David Hockney was wearing two hearing aids, one in each ear, and I asked him about them.

'My hearing loss was having an effect – I was getting more antisocial, in a way, because I just couldn't hear people – and it was getting worse. Sounds were getting both dimmer and more blurred. So in 1984 I went to some specialists, and they all told me the same thing, that it would continue to get gradually worse, there was nothing you could do to arrest it, but that a more sophisticated hearing aid would help. So I got one, and the moment I put it on, it was like a big muffler had been taken off my head. The guy had said either ear would do since they're both the same. So I went back to him and said, "I think I'll take two." He said not too many people put two on; they think it looks too bad, makes you look old. I said, "I don't really care what it looks like. I'd rather hear." I mean, I'm not vain in that way. I wanted him to make me a red one and a blue one.'

Mismatched. Like his socks.

'I mean,' he continued, 'you'd have to be daft to think that nobody's going to notice it. But who cares? People come up to me now, and they ask, "Have you got hearing problems?" and I say, "Well I used to have, but I don't now." It's made a world of difference. Everybody comments on how my body movements have changed: I don't lean over, I can lie back and listen, I don't have to be watching people's faces, lip-reading.'

Ray Charles White, *Daily Telegraph Magazine*, 29.10.88, interview with Hockney

★ ★ ★

If you aren't worrying, you don't know the problem.

★ ★ ★

But, Jesus, when you don't have any money, the problem is food. When you have money, it's sex. When you have both, it's health ... if everything is simply jake then you're frightened of death.

J P Donleavy, *The Ginger Man*, quoted in *Guardian*, 29.12.89, page 22

★ ★ ★

30 September 1811 – Fanny Burney, suffering from breast cancer, describes her mastectomy: 'When the dreadful steel was plunged into the breast – cutting through veins, arteries, flesh, nerves, I needed no injunctions not to restrain my cries. I began a scream that lasted unintermittently during the whole time of the incision & I almost marvel that it rings not in my ears still! so excruciating was the agony. When the wound was made, & the instrument was withdrawn, the pain seemed undiminished, for the air that rushed into those delicate parts felt like a mass of minute but sharp-forked poniards, that were tearing the edge of the wound – but when again I felt the instrument ... then, indeed, I thought I must have expired.'

A Day Like This, *Independent*, 30.9.93

★ ★ ★

A supervisor at a firm with a strict no-smoking policy has been sacked for allegedly lighting a cigarette in his car as he left at the end of a night shift. A video camera at the factory – which supplies materials to the tobacco industry – recorded a flash of light in the car. John Dixon, 54, denies the misdemeanour and is taking a claim of unfair dismissal to an industrial tribunal. John Goodridge, branch officer of the Graphical, Paper and Media union, which is supporting the tribunal claim, said: 'First of all he denies he was smoking and, even if he was, the infringement was so slight. It was twenty minutes after he had finished his shift, he was in his car and it can only have been two or three seconds before he got through the gate.'

Michael Horsnell, *The Times*, 28.8.98

# Laughter is Sudden Glory

*(Laughter and Humour)*

Don't stop me if you've heard this one before. There is no reason why a joke should not be appreciated more than once. Imagine how little good music there would be if, for example, a conductor refused to play Beethoven's Fifth Symphony on the grounds that his audience might have heard it before.

A P Herbert

★  ★  ★

Just once, at a dinner party, I heard an original pun delivered with such speed and spontaneity that not only did the table break up with laughter, but I have never forgotten the joke. We were talking about a young woman who, after some years of dallying with penniless artists, had finally upped and married a young man in the City. Quick as a flash came the line: 'This is the way the girls end: not with a whim, but with a banker.'

Angela Lambert, *Independent*, 31.12.88

★  ★  ★

'How would you like to talk to your mother-in-law?'
'Through a spiritualist.'

★  ★  ★

I've always been obsessed by the idea of 'What is a laugh?' As a child I used to haunt libraries, reading everything I could on the nature of comedy. How did it work? What made one man funnier than another? And after all these years I've come to the conclusion that somewhere there exists a little comic spirit, a muse if you like – something that is quite apart from personality and technique.

I first sensed this when I was sixteen and I went to see Frank Randle play Wishee-Washee in *Aladdin* at the Liverpool Theatre of Varieties. Aristotle said that the essence of comedy is a buckled millwheel, meaning that it is everyday life out of true, and Randle had this; he was a genius. He was also a grotesque. He had a face like a medieval gargoyle. When he came onstage for the first time he simply stood and gaped at the audience with this terrible leer. And the audience shrieked with laughter for fully five minutes. Randle didn't say a word. He just stood and stared at them. It was quite incredible.

Because he looked the way he did, Randle used to collect strange people. If he saw someone with a misshaped nose or ear then he'd sign them up and take them away with him. He supported this whole entourage of grotesques. Eventually he had so many that he had to find something for them to do, so he grouped them together and called them the Mandalay Singers and had them standing in the middle of the stage. Behind them was this backcloth of a street in old Peking, while Randle, dressed as Wishee-Washee in his little smock, thrashed about wildly in the orchestra pit conducting them in the Hallelujah Chorus. Fabulous stuff, absolutely inspired.

Ken Dodd, *Sunday Telegraph*, 4.11.90, page 13

\* \* \*

Most comedy is the perception of incongruity.

Ken Dood, quoting Aristotle, *Sunday Times Magazine*, 28.4.91

\* \* \*

An ostrich came across a group of other ostriches all with their heads in the sand. 'Where on earth is every*body*?' he exclaimed.

\* \* \*

Giving evidence in a murder case, the constable reported: 'She had multiple stab wounds in her head and chest. Both her legs had been cut off. But, your worship, she had not been interfered with.'

★ ★ ★

Barry Sheen, the racing driver, has had two legs broken and a severe fracture of an upper arm. The hospital reports that he is comfortable.
Radio report, July 1982

★ ★ ★

One rattlesnake said to another, 'I'm poisoned, I just bit my tongue.'

★ ★ ★

Hello, handsome. Can you tell me the way to an optician?
Roy Fell

★ ★ ★

My grandfather was killed at Custer's last stand. He was camping in the next field and went over to complain about the noise.
Roy Fell

★ ★ ★

An elephant seeing a naked man for the first time says, 'You don't mean to tell me you breathe through that?'
Larry Adler, *What's On*, 10.4.81

★ ★ ★

Two little girls saw a naked little boy having a bath and one said to the other, 'It's lucky it doesn't grow on his face.'

★ ★ ★

Exit pursued by a bear.
Shakespeare, *Winter's Tale*

★ ★ ★

A milkmaid haunts me.
Sung by bearded lady in Auden and Stravinsky's *Rake's Progress*

# Kill All the Lawyers!
*(Law)*

Lawyers are the only persons in whom ignorance of the law is not punished.
Jeremy Bentham

\* \* \*

In comparative law there are four fundamental principles to be recognized: in England everything is permitted that is not legally forbidden; in Germany everything is forbidden that is not legally permitted; in the Soviet Union everything is forbidden, even that which is legally permitted; and in France everything is permitted, even that which is legally forbidden.
David Daube, international lawyer, *Punch*, 31.8.77

\* \* \*

When a judge in an abrasive exchange with the famous barrister F E Smith told him: 'You are extremely offensive, young man,' Smith replied: 'As a matter of fact we both are. The only difference is that I am trying to be and you cannot help it.'
Fenton Bresler, *Daily Mail*, 21.10.83, page 7

\* \* \*

Lawyers are rarely popular. Generally they are wise to remain in a state of total obscurity since if they ever emerge it is usually to enjoy some deserved opprobrium.
Arnold Goodman, reviewing *What Next in the Law* by Lord Denning,
*Sunday Times*, 8.8.82

\* \* \*

Q:  What do you call two hundred lawyers at the bottom of
    the sea?
A:  A good start.

★ ★ ★

Laws are like cobwebs, which may catch small flies but let
wasps and hornets break through.
Jonathan Swift

★ ★ ★

That a majority, merely because it is a majority, should be
entitled to apply to a minority a rule that does not apply to
itself is an infringement of a principle much more fundamental
than democracy itself, a principle on which the justification of
democracy rests.
Friedrich Hayek

★ ★ ★

When Jeffrey Bernard's mother was found guilty of 'contempt
of court', she told the magistrate, 'Make that "utter".'

★ ★ ★

American lawyers may be regarded as even more repulsive than
journalists, but their reputation for mental sharpness knows few
boundaries. For a collation of some of the most acute questions
asked lately in New England courtrooms, we are indebted to
the *Journal of the Massachusetts Bar* and we begin today with the
following exchange, between anonymous attorney and
pathologist, from a recent murder trial.

'Doctor, before you performed the autopsy, did you check
for a pulse?'

'No.'

'Did you check for breathing?'

'No.'

'So then, is it possible that the patient was alive when you began the autopsy?'

'No.'

'How can you be so sure?'

'Because his brain was sitting on my desk in a jar.'

Even then, this would-be Barry Sheck refused to throw in the towel: 'Is it possible the patient could have been alive nevertheless?'

'It is possible that he could have been alive,' said the pathologist, 'and practising law somewhere.'

# Excuse My Dust

*(Life and Death, Last Words and Epitaphs)*

Life can only be understood backwards, but it must be lived forwards.

Kierkegaard

\* \* \*

It is difficult to commit suicide when you are in need of a pee.

Milton Shulman

\* \* \*

As a last wish Reginald Johnson, who died two decades ago, and was the Scots tutor of China's last emperor Pu Yi, asked that his ashes be scattered over Loch Craignish, Argyllshire, to the sound of the bagpipes.

A Piper McLaren was duly summoned to blow the lament, but while he took a deep breath, the strong wind blew the ashes in his face.

'Good God,' wailed the piper, 'I've swallowed Sir Reginald.'

Ross Benson, *Daily Express*, 8.4.88, page 19

\* \* \*

If that man ran a funeral parlour, nobody would die.

Line of dialogue from the film *Wall Street*, 1988

\* \* \*

What fascinates New York commodity futures traders more than the consumer price index? The health or otherwise of celebrated movie stars and politicians, apparently. The hundred members of the Great Beyond have been winning and losing money for the past couple of years according to the timing of the various big-name appointments with St Peter.

It works like this. Each trader pays ten dollars up front to join, and a five dollar monthly membership fee thereafter. He or she gets allocated a celebrity by picking names from a hat. Whoever's celebrity dies next scoops the pool. To qualify, the famous persons – ranging from Mother Teresa to Gene Kelly – have to be over fifty and not too well. Excitement is running high at the moment because 'no one' has died for three months so there is about $2,500 in the kitty.

Observer, *Financial Times*, 1.8.94

\* \* \*

What would you do if you had only a few hours to live? Or even a few minutes? George Steiner (as one might expect) supplies the prize-winning example: the French duke who, while in the tumbrel, was seen to be reading a book. Arriving at the steps of the guillotine, he turned down the corner of his text, as if for a temporary absence, and took the steps to the Great Library in the Sky. Are such things possible in a classless society?

Frederic Raphael, *Spectator*, 19.1.91

\* \* \*

When a priest asked Voltaire on his deathbed to renounce the Devil, the sage replied, 'This is no time to risk losing friends.'

\* \* \*

> I had written to Aunt Maud,
> Who was on a trip abroad,
> When I heard she'd died of cramp—
> Just too late to save the stamp.

Harry Graham, quoted in *Comic Muse* by J C Squire

\* \* \*

David Niven's first wife, Primula, died after falling down some cellar steps whilst playing 'Sardines' at a Hollywood dinner party. She has been attributed with the politely touching last words, 'They'll never ask us again.'

Sheridan Morley's biography of Niven, *The Other Side of the Moon*, in the *Sunday Times*, 1.9.85

\* \* \*

Tell them that the pain is on the left side.

George Eliot, author of *Middlemarch*

\* \* \*

'Could you shut up, please!' were the last words of cartoonist Mel Calman when, watching the film *Carlito's Way*, in February 1994 in the Empire Cinema, Leicester Square, he was irritated by a chattering couple behind him. He collapsed and died soon after.

\* \* \*

You will find my last words in the blue folder on my desk.

Max Beerbohm, quoted in a letter in *Spectator*, 8.4.95

\* \* \*

I have always thought that having 'That's all, folks' engraved on one's tombstone would be amusing. However, when I mentioned this to fellow cartoonist Michael Ffolks, he demanded that he have it. So I let it go. When I first sent my work to *Punch*, they used to reject my drawing with the words, 'Not quite – try again.' I think I'll use that as my epitaph.

Michael Heath, My Week, *Independent* 1.9.88

\* \* \*

God caught his eye.
Epitaph for a waiter

\* \* \*

God spiked his copy.
Epitaph for a journalist, Milton Shulman

\* \* \*

Excuse my dust.
Robert Benchley

\* \* \*

He practised no religion, which is why he died laughing.
Own epitaph by Benny Green (broadcaster and musician)

\* \* \*

Words on the tombstone above the grave of a frustrated playwright: 'A plot at last.'

\* \* \*

Dorothy Parker requested that her tombstone bear her name and the words: 'I am here against my better judgement.'
Peterborough, *Daily Telegraph*, 26.7.94

\* \* \*

There is one Victorian tombstone whose stern legend keeps forcing itself upon my attention:

> As you pass by, so once was I.
> As I am now, so you will be,
> Therefore, prepare for eternity.

This started off a memory train that led me to request from Dublin the verse a friend found long ago in a death notice. He demanded full attribution, so thanks to Professor Ronan Fanning for:

> The heavenly trumpets sounded,
> St Peter called out 'Come',
> The Pearly Gates flew open
> And in walked Mum.

Ruth Dudley Edwards, *Guardian*, 10.4.95

★ ★ ★

There was no fear in her except for me.

Reflection on the death of his mother in Noël Coward's *Diaries*, page 239

★ ★ ★

On Sunday 5 April 1998, following a courageous fight for life, Catherine Thomas (née Holder) surrounded by family, died at home – 'and she's bloody annoyed!'

Notice in Cardiff local paper, April 1998

# Words Fail Me
*(Words and Language)*

## Typographical Blunders at the *Evening Standard*

'Olfactory sense' came out as 'old factory fence'

'Brahms waltzes' came out as 'brass horses' (music review, 1986)

'Bored disc jockey' came out as 'bald disc jockey' (in *Angry Housewife* review, Milton Shulman, 30.4.86)

'Haughty Malvolio' came out as 'naughty Malvolio' (review of *Twelfth Night*, Milton Shulman)

The *Evening Standard* had on tape a news story about an accident to a 'twenty-seven-year-old rigger'. It came across on the tape as 'twenty-seven-year-old nigger'. The sub-editor, conscious of race-relations law, changed it to 'twenty-seven-year-old West Indian'. (June 1987)

\* \* \*

A *Times* journalist tells me that when he referred to the Dead Sea Scrolls they emerged as 'Dead Sea Squirrels'.

\* \* \*

The editor would like to point out a printer's error in last month's paper, which had 'allegories of Jesus' rendered as 'allergies of Jesus'.

Apology in the *Beacon*, parish magazine for Brecon and District

Take back your mini.

\* \* \*

In *The Times* review of *Guys and Dolls*, instead of 'mink'. 4.3.82

\* \* \*

Review of opera *Doris Gudonov*

\* \* \*

The *Sound of Music* is a monument to the 'impotence' of critics. Came out as 'impudence'.
Milton Shulman, review, 1982

\* \* \*

Review of Skylark instead of Shylock.
Philip Hope-Wallace

\* \* \*

Philip Hope-Wallace, music critic, telephoned an opera notice to his paper in which he described the leading lady as 'like a tigress robbed of her whelps'. The lady sub-editor, a women's libber, changed the word 'tigress' to 'tiger'. The printer then accidentally changed 'whelps' to 'whelks'. The resultant notice had a soprano described as 'a tiger robbed of his whelks'.
Alan Watkins, *Brief Lives*

\* \* \*

An American newspaper editor ran an item in his paper announcing a major new appointment at 'Manufacturers Hanover Trust, a large baking concern'. When the angry letter from the aggrieved bankers duly arrived the editor replied, 'The easy way out would be to blame the mistake on a typographical error. The truth of the matter, however, is that

our reporter was under the mistaken impression that the name of your company was Manufacturers Hanover Crust.'
*Financial Times*, 23.9.82

★ ★ ★

*Apology:* The first sentence of Friday's sketch, 'God lives with his shadow,' may have struck you as either the most meaningful new thought in Western philosophy or as evidence that I have gone stark raving mad.

Despite its subtle, plangent quality, I must disavow this *pensée*. It was produced by my computer omitting the following italicised words: 'God*frey Barker, Commons Sketch. Every minister* lives with his shadow.

Perhaps my little Japanese deserves a PhD for a piercing insight. Sadly, it is going back to Tokyo for surgery.
Commons Sketch, Godfrey Barker, *Daily Telegraph*, 21.7.87

★ ★ ★

An apology appears in this week's edition of the House of Commons magazine: 'In the profile of Doug Hoyle, MP, last week, a most unfortunate error occurred. It left out the italicized words below. The text should have read: "My mother died when I was sixteen, but my father didn't disapprove *of my joining the Labour Party*."'
*Independent*, 27.11.87, page 19

★ ★ ★

Words to avoid because typesetters, feature subs or proof-readers always change them:

Causal becomes casual
Marital becomes martial
Eclectic becomes electric

★ ★ ★

Sir – Twenty years ago you told us that Sir Malcolm Sargent was a master at controlling chairs. On 4 June, at last, you have put the record straight, by reporting that a choir had been thrown through a window.

Yours, etc., Fritz Spiegl, Liverpool

Letter to *Guardian*, 6.6.85

★ ★ ★

In the course of writing *Clarendon and His Friends*, to be published in September, the historian Richard Ollard has corrected an unfortunate misprint that had gone undetected for centuries.

Clarendon, Charles II's Lord Chancellor, describing a visit to Avignon in his memoirs, had in every printed edition been made to observe: 'The ill savour of the streets by the multitude of dyers and of the silk manufacturers, and the worse smell of the Jews, made him doubt that it could be no pleasant place to make an abode in during the heat of summer.'

It seemed to Ollard out of character that a man so liberal and humane as Clarendon – and one well versed in Jewish history and literature – should have descended to vulgar anti-Semitism. Robert Latham, the former Pepys Librarian at Magdalene College, Cambridge, when invited to read Ollard's new book in typescript, suggest that 'Jews' could be a misreading of 'stews' – an archaic name for brothels. So the author went back to Clarendon's original manuscript. There he found that the word was 'sewers'.

It is an episode from which all three historians emerge with credit.

Albany, *Sunday Telegraph*, 28.6.87

★ ★ ★

My distinguished Aunt Anna had a house on the west coast of Cork and always spoke with affection of the simple, straightforward decency of the local people. She was in Skibereen for her seventieth birthday and received hundreds of telegrams of goodwill from all parts of the world where psychoanalysis rules OK. The messages were telephoned through to the postmistress, who inscribed them on greetings forms and hired a boy to deliver them hourly to the Freud house. During the afternoon she received one which read: 'The rapists of Philadelphia send good wishes and best regards.' Over which my elderly maiden aunt puzzled greatly. When she called on the postmistress the next day she asked if they might send off for verification. The postmistress said that she, too, had been shocked by the words and checked them, and they had been right. Therapists is not a word in common usage around those parts.

Clement Freud, *The Times*, 8.8.88, page 10

\* \* \*

Lord Ribbesdale, the 'Picturesque Peer' painted in Sargent's best manner at the Tate Gallery, told me, when I was too young to believe him, that it was gentlemanly to get one's quotations very slightly wrong. In that way one unprigged oneself and allowed the company to correct one.

Lady Diana Manners, *Autobiography*, quoted in a letter to *The Times*, 26.5.83

\* \* \*

We were talking over Sunday lunch about the funny things that happen to people on trains and John Piper came up with the following story. Some time about the beginning of the war the art critic Eric Newton was travelling in a compartment with a young girl who had with her a very large suitcase. At some time during the journey the girl took down the case and opened it. Newton was amazed to see that it was entirely filled with lemons – then impossible to buy in Britain. The girl offered him two which he accepted gratefully. No further conversation took place between the two of them but towards the end of the journey he presented his fellow traveller with one of his books that he happened to have with him, inscribing it: 'A poor exchange for two lemons. Eric Newton.' Some years passed and one day Newton received a letter out of the blue: 'Dear Mr Newton, you once inscribed a book to my daughter with the words "A poor exchange for two lemons." Would you kindly explain what you meant by this?' To which Newton replied: 'When I wrote, "A poor exchange for two lemons", I meant exactly what I said.' He heard no more.

*The Spectator*, 5.10.85

* * *

A Sidmouth reader assures me, she heard this intriguing exchange in an operating theatre anteroom.

    Doctor: 'Why do you want to be sterilized?'
    Woman: 'Well, you see, my husband is a cricketer.'

Peterborough, *Daily Telegraph*, 3.9.88

* * *

Overheard conversation in a Cambridge college court with one don saying to another, 'And ninthly...'

*Financial Times*, 29.1.88, page 22

* * *

From Australia I am indebted to the man who overheard a lady at *Madame Butterfly* in the war saying to her friend, 'Of course, since Pearl Harbor one can't feel nearly so sorry for her.'

Sheridan Morley, *The Times*, 24.8.88

* * *

'Blackmail,' said Bradley 'Ardacre (an 'ard man in an 'ard hat), 'is an ugly word.'

I don't see it myself. Quite euphonious, I would have thought. Not half as ugly as scuttle or wattle or psoriasis or sopition or anfractuosity.

Nancy Banks-Smith reviewing TV programme *Brass*, *Guardian*, 22.5.84

\* \* \*

Language is the mirror of events. Our language is having to adapt fast to reflect the tremendous changes in the old Soviet empire... Soviet, one of the most popular and terrible words in our lexicon for seventy years, has now passed into the overmatter of history, along with Witenagenot and Star Chamber... in the English the name Commonwealth is heavily loaded with Oliver Cromwell and Roundheads. In America, Commonwealth forms part of the official titles of Kentucky, Massachusetts, Pennsylvania and Virginia. Considerable confusion lies ahead if we start talking about the Russian Commonwealth. Confusion is the element through which language ploughs, like an icebreaker in freezing fog.

Philip Howard, *The Times*, 11.1.92, page 10.

\* \* \*

It's our monthly Scribblers' Lunch today at the Chelsea Arts Club, and although seven of us write regular newspaper columns none has yet come up with the right collective noun. What should it be? A Parthenon of columnists? A pillar? A pomposity? Other groups of scribblers are much easier: a chapter of authors; a percentage of agents; a remainder of publishers; a rumour of diarists; a shrivel of critics. Best of all, though, is the collective noun for jockeys. They are known as a shortage.

\* \* \*

No way; hopefully; nitty gritty; area; situation; tummy; process; loo; object of the exercise; at the end of the day; light at the end of the tunnel; in point of fact; to be perfectly honest; y'know; like; serious criticism; what's that in aid of; as it were; if you like; when all that's been said; at this moment of time; ordinary citizens; not in the same ball game; victory for common sense.

List by Larry Holm of clichés of 1981 from *What's On*, 8.1.82

\* \* \*

A visitor to an American-run research station complimented his hosts on the windows in the computer suite. 'Those aren't windows,' he was told. 'They're environment-awareness panels.'

Observer, *Financial Times*, 20.3.90

# Till Death Us Do Part

*(Marriage, Love and Hate)*

Marriage is based on the theory that when a man discovers a brand of beer exactly to his taste, he should at once throw up his job and go to work in the brewery.

George Jean Nathan, 1958

\* \* \*

Paying alimony is like feeding hay to a dead horse.

Groucho Marx

\* \* \*

On the death of her husband, his widow was inconsolable. She wept for three days incessantly. When the insurance company's agent turned up with a cheque for £50,000 on her husband's insurance her tears dried up. 'You won't believe it,' she said to the agent, 'but I would gladly give up £20,000 of this to have him back.'

\* \* \*

Kingsley Amis, the writer, during his fourteen-year marriage to Elizabeth Jane Howard used to say, 'I'm older and heavier and I earn more money,' whenever he wanted his own way – and he wanted it most of the time.

Elizabeth Jane Howard interviewed by Lynda Lee-Potter, *Daily Mail*, 25.7.82

\* \* \*

When in 1892 Beatrice Potter married Sidney Webb (both dedicated socialists) he gave her a wedding ring inscribed (according to their best friend, Bernard Shaw) '*Pro bono publico*' or 'In the public interest'. 'And,' said Shaw darkly, 'this was no idle threat.'

Hilary Spurling, *Evening Standard*, 19.10.83

\* \* \*

Why does the Pygmy
Indulge in polygmy?
His tribal dogma
Frowns on monogma.

Ogden Nash, *Third Jungle Book*, quoted by Godfrey Smith in the *Sunday Times*, 13.3.88

\* \* \*

The claims of marriage are so heavy that it often takes more than two to bear them.

La Rochefoucauld

\* \* \*

I think men who have a pierced ear are better prepared for marriage. They've experienced pain and bought jewellery.

Rita Rudner in *The Book of Lists – the '90s Edition* by David Wallechinsky and Amy Wallace (Aurum Press)

\* \* \*

By all means get married. If you get a good wife, you'll be happy. If you get a bad one, you'll become a philosopher.

Socrates, ibid.

\* \* \*

Married men live longer than single men. But married men are a lot more willing to die.

Johnny Carson, ibid.

★ ★ ★

In Sir Thomas More's *Utopia* his lawe is that the young people are to see each other stark naked before marriage. Sir William Roper, of Eltham in Kent, came one morning pretty early, to my lord, with a proposall to marry one of his daughters. My lord's daughters were then both together abed in a truckle-bed in their father's chamber asleep. He carries Sir William into the chamber and takes the sheete by the corner and suddenly whippes it off. They lay on their backs and their smocks up as high as their armpits. This awakened them, and immediately they turned on their bellies. Quoth Roper, 'I have seen both sides,' and so giving a patt on her Buttock he made choice (of Margaret) saying 'Thou art mine.'

John Aubrey, *Brief Lives*

★ ★ ★

When you marry a mistress you create a job vacancy.

Sir James Goldsmith (tycoon), *Evening Standard*, 18.7.89, page 19

★ ★ ★

It's a club, you know, and a sort of secret society. Either you are a born member or you are not. And somehow I don't think I ever was. I was scared of disease, conception, involvement, retribution and, above all, my own physical incompetence. To be a member of the club, one must have no such fears.

Robert Morley, quoted by Sheridan Morley in his biography of his father.

★ ★ ★

President Coolidge and his wife were visiting a government farm. Passing the chicken coops, Mrs Coolidge enquired how often the rooster made love each day. 'Dozens of times,' was the reply. 'Please tell that to the president,' she said. When he passed the pen and was told about the rooster, he asked, 'Same hen every time?' 'Oh no, Mr President, a different one each time.' Coolidge nodded slowly, 'Please tell that to Mrs Coolidge.'
Ned Sherrin, *The Times*, 11.11.89

\* \* \*

Christianity has done a great deal for love by making a sin of it.
Anatole France, *Book of Aphorisms*

\* \* \*

Beryl de Zoete, first wife of the sinologist Arthur Waley, was a skilled belly dancer who apparently had an aversion to sex. Her first love affair was consummated when she and her young man, swinging nude in adjacent poplar trees, made their branches, but not their persons, touch.
Review by Piers Brindon of *A Half of Two Lives* by Alison Waley, *Observer*, 12.9.82

\* \* \*

> You reached over (horizontally)
> And took the phone. You rang
> Your husband, and you said
> I shall not be home. And, I am
> Not alone.
> I loved you. But what hating
> Made you, over me, your breast
> Touching my own, most graceful
> One, reach to the phone?

Geoffrey Grigson, *Collected Poems 1963–80* (Allison & Busby)

\* \* \*

Love is, sooner or later, the beginning of all suffering.
Wolf Dietrich von Raitenau, Archbishop of Salzburg, 1611

\* \* \*

I knew that in many cases it is a mistake to pay too much attention to the appearance of people one saw in one's dream, who may perhaps have been disguised or have exchanged faces...the person whom we love is to be recognized only by the intensity of the pain we suffer.
Marcel Proust, *Within a Budding Grove,* (1918)

# Behave Yourself
## (Manners)

Manners are the lowest common denominator of ethical experience.

Victor Navasky in Jonathan Green's *Says Why?*

\* \* \*

A post office sorter came across a letter addressed simply, 'God, Heaven'. He opened it and found a letter from a seventy-five-year-old widow saying, 'Dear God, you are my last hope. I have an electricity bill for ninety-six pounds which I cannot pay. Can you help?' The sorter was touched by the letter and showed it to his colleagues. They had a whip-round and raised ninety pounds. They put it in an envelope and sent it off to the woman anonymously.

A week later another letter arrived addressed, 'God, Heaven'. The sorter opened it. It was a thank you note from the widow saying she had received the ninety pounds. 'As you know,' the letter went on, 'the bill was for ninety-six pounds, but I suppose those thieving so-and-so's in the Post Office pinched six pounds out of the letter.'

*Financial Times*, quoting the *Irish Times*, 10.9.84, page 18

\* \* \*

The students call me a fascist. That's because I don't think they should steal books from the library.

Philip Larkin, quoted by Geoffrey Wheatcroft, 9.8.82

\* \* \*

It is hard to believe that a man is telling the truth when you know that you would lie if you were in his place.
H L Mencken

\* \* \*

> She would have lived her life
> In nonchalance and insouciance
> But for earning her living
> Which was rather a nuisance.

Ogden Nash

\* \* \*

The family is the only consistently subversive organism, dividing society and putting private before communal good, and consequently it has always aroused the hostility of intellectuals and nominal subversives – Utopians, feminists, hippies, Jesus, Marx, Lenin, Mao, Hitler – everyone in fact, who wants to control and change the way people live.
John Carey, reviewing Ferdinand Mount's book *The Subversive Family*,
*Sunday Times*, 18.7.82

\* \* \*

The only pleasure in life equal to that of being called on to make an after-dinner speech is the one of not being called on to make one.

\* \* \*

When a man opens the car door for his wife, it's either a new car or a new wife.
Prince Philip, quoted in Sayings of the Week, *Observer*, 6.3.88 page, 15

\* \* \*

Spike Milligan, the comedian, was once asked by an acquaintance why everyone took an instant dislike to him. 'It saves time,' replied Spike.

BBC 2, 8.11.83

\* \* \*

Years ago, during one of my few appearances on horseback, I was trying to impress a lady companion with both my horsemanship and intellect. During a lull in the conversation my horse farted audibly. Having no knowledge of the etiquette in such circumstances I apologized hesitatingly to the lady. 'It's quite all right,' she retorted, 'I thought it was the horse.'

Letter from Jem Cook of Marlborough, Wilts, in the *Spectator*, 21.4.84, page 17

\* \* \*

This Earle of Oxford, making of his low obeisance to Queen Elizabeth, happened to let a fart, at which he was so abashed and ashamed that he went to travell, seven yeares. On his return the Queen welcomed him home and sayd, 'My lord, I had quite forgott the fart.'

John Aubrey's *Brief Life of Edward De Vere, Earl of Oxford*, quoted in letter in the *Spectator*, 28.4.84

\* \* \*

When Beau Brummel was once congratulated on his elegance, he replied crossly that if he had been noticed, then he couldn't have been elegant.

\* \* \*

I always carry a black tie in my bag since I was stranded in Khartoum in 1945 at the death of Queen Mary.

Philip Hope-Wallace

\* \* \*

No good deed ever goes unpunished.
Clare Boothe Luce

·  ★ ★ ★

The ballet critic Richard Buckle once said of Dame Margot Fonteyn that she was so infuriatingly well brought up, 'she would never, even under torture, admit that pink was her favourite colour for fear of offending orange and mauve'.
Margot Norman, *Daily Telegraph*, 18.11.87, page 11

★ ★ ★

## Antiphone

hello is that you look I just
wanted to say for
my sake as much as
yours things I have not
said but should have and so should
you things our ones would not
say to your ones in case
your ones might be you know
the kind of thing your ones
would hide from
our ones for your ones
were always a bit
crafty you know sleekid even
not mind you that I blame
you personally considering
you know what we all know
about you know who though
god knows you couldn't have
known but then there was always
that streak in them not like

us if it has to be said better
to say it out I say and
be done better to call a spade a
whatyoumaycallit and not be
beatin about the
thingimybob you have to know exactly
where you stand which is why
I'm glad I've said
what I've said so I am.

Tomás Ó Canainn, *Spectator*, 4.7.87

\* \* \*

The latest example of broken humanity to upset me was a
waiter at a training restaurant I'd decided to patronise on
account of its cheap lunches. Soup of the day for the price of
a box of matches; chicken à l'Indochine with house rice for
the price of a cappuccino – how could I say no? OK, so the
service was going to be a bit on the gauche side. And there'd
be a tutor hovering near, muttering, 'Not like that, like this,'
while my tongue hung out, but so what? It would be nice not
to be looked down on by a waiter for a change. What I hadn't
realized was how gauche gauche can get. The poor bastard's
hands shook more than mine did. He tripped over his own leg.
He didn't know where to put anything, the knives, the spoons,
himself. He had a long, fashionably lugubrious face
(fashionable on someone who knew how to stay upright), an
ear-ring which didn't become him, and he was past the age of
learning.

I knew better than to ask for wine. Wine would have been
too cruel. But I made the mistake of saying yes to iced water.
And how did he pour it? With his non-pouring hand behind
his back! Five hundred smackers to be taught what they do in
the world's thousand least sophisticated restaurants. The last
time anyone poured me a drink with his non-pouring hand

behind his back was in a once, but no longer, grand café in Kaunas, in Lithuania. The waiter wore stained livery, which was meant to compensate for the fact of there being nothing on the menu except the menu itself schnitzeled, and nothing to drink except sweet white urine of Tartary mountain yak (and I happen to have an aversion to it sweet). Not that it mattered. I'd only gone in to use the lavatory.

Howard Jacobson, *Independent Magazine*, 31.8.98

# The Way We Are
*(Modern Living)*

I have a cheering prediction for candidates on the forth-coming French presidential elections. The voters will believe just about anything. This much is apparent from a revealing anecdote in a book called *Forbidden Knowledge: The Paranormal Paradox* by Bob Couttie about a mischievous French psychologist who advertised a free, ten-page 'ultra personal' horoscope in a magazine. He received five hundred replies.

Each respondent received, along with the horoscope, a questionnaire. It emerged that ninety-four per cent thought the horoscope accurate; ninety per cent of their friends and family thought the same. There was a catch: the psychologist sent exactly the same horoscope to everyone. It was based on a sensitive, right-minded middle class subject called Dr Petiot. Coincidentally, Dr Petiot was also a notorious mass murderer.

\* \* \*

When all else fails, read the instructions.

\* \* \*

Sir – Your correspondent, Leonard Cook, who was unable to open his eyedrops or margarine without mechanical help, was yet another victim of a secret organization known as the PPPC (People-Proof Packaging Corporation) which has been acting as consultant to British industry for many years past.

One of PPPC's earliest creations was the pre-packed butter pat, half of which remained on the wrapper. It then took a giant step forward with the exploding cream capsule for coffee, which led in turn to the unopenable milk carton, the miniature jam cocoon, the mustard or mayonnaise sachet and the plastic casings widely used for everything from razor-blades and toothbrushes to electric batteries and carpenters' screws. All of these have become marvellously simple to transport, store and display, but impossible for the consumer to open without blood, sweat and tears.

Gerald Priestland, London NW11

Letter to *The Times*, 24.12.87

\* \* \*

A reader in Kent assures us that this story is true. A man was driving home from a party, stopped by the police and about to be breath-tested when there was an accident on the other side of the motorway. The police told him he was 'bloody lucky' and to drive carefully. Then they crossed the road to attend to the accident.

A few hours later he was aroused from his sleep by the police at his front door. They asked if he owned a car with a certain registration number. He said 'yes', picked up his keys and unlocked his garage. There was a police car inside.

*Financial Times*, 25.3.88

\* \* \*

If you remember the sixties, you weren't there.

George Harrison

\* \* \*

Person to work on nuclear fissionable isotope molecular reactive counters and three phase cyclotronic uranium photo-synthesisers. No experience necessary.

Help-wanted advertisement in a Miami newspaper quoted in a book on the Peter Principle

\* \* \*

I have seen people who hate being famous, detest recognition and slink down alleyways rather than meet a member of the public, and I have seen others who revel in the limelight, adore being spotted and positively glow when stopped in the street. I cannot argue that one position is morally superior to the other. The real drawback with television celebrity, as far a my own humble share of it is concerned, is that it prevents me from ever showing annoyance at terrible service in a restaurant or from tutting with impatience in a supermarket queue. One has to face life's irritations with a benign and foolish grin all over one's face. Otherwise one will be accused of expecting special attention. Gone are the days when one could rap on the counter and demand to see the manager.

I realized that something was psychically wrong with this whole business of celebrity when I first noticed, some years ago, that the hands of an autograph hunter waiting for me at a stage door shook like a blancmange as she handed over her book to be signed. Talking to people who had been longer in the public eye, I discovered that this is very, very common. It sounds insane, I know, but there are people who quiver and tremble from head to foot simply because they are in my presence. This is wildly disturbing and disquieting. That the fame which adventitiously accompanies certain professions can have such an effect must be unhealthy. If it were a reaction confined to teenage girls I suppose one could draw bracing and obvious conclusions, but it is not. Our whole culture seems to have gone fame crazy.

Stephen Fry, *Daily Telegraph*, 22.3.91

\* \* \*

Sir, I wonder if any of your readers can help me. I am thinking of setting up a twenty-four-hour helpline for people who have absolutely nothing wrong with them. Although only a tiny minority, these people have to cope daily with the knowledge that they alone have no one to ring up and tell their troubles to (what with not having any in the first place).

I feel there is a definite need for short-term, medium-term and long-term counselling to help these unfortunates overcome their sense of deprivation and isolation in the community. Could any of your readers give me the number of the particular twenty-four-hour helpline which gives advice to others on how to set up a twenty-four-hour helpline?

Yours etc., Henry Thompson, Llangollen, Clwyd

Letter to *The Times*, 22.2.92

\* \* \*

Intellectuals tend to hold contempt for cars. It cannot be an accident that the most highly educated, poetical, artistic and generally fancy people are also the group with the highest proportion of non-drivers. I doubt if there is a bank manager in Britain who cannot drive (no letters from exceptions to this rule, please), but non-driving is one of the badges of the creative artist. This is not a matter of convenience – bank managers do not need to move about, artists frequently do – but a question of conviction, or at least of disposition.

To a person who thinks of himself as creative, eccentric, individual, the car symbolizes the herd instinct, the indistinguishable mass, the people who do things simply because everyone else does them. The car is the emblem of the century of the common man, with all its uniformity and trivial comfort.

Charles Moore, editor of the *Spectator*, *Daily Telegraph*, 11.8.87

\* \* \*

Humour is tolerant, tender, its ridicule caresses; wit stabs, begs pardon – and turns the weapon in the wound.

Ambrose Bierce, *New Statesman*, 21.11.83, page 23

\* \* \*

A joke is an epitaph on an emotion.

Nietzsche

* * *

Impotence and sodomy are socially OK but birth control is flagrantly middle class.

Evelyn Waugh

* * *

This matter of the gross inequality which now disfigures our society's arrangements in relation to supernatural phenomena was first brought to my attention by a gentleman who, some years ago, mounted a campaign in favour of more working class ghosts, observing correctly that, in this class-ridden community of ours, ghosts are drawn almost exclusively from the ranks of the rich and privileged.

T E Utley, *Daily Telegraph*, 24.12.84

* * *

When the sixth Duke of Somerset (1662–1748) on one occasion felt his second wife tapping him lightly with her fan, he turned to her with the imperious rebuke: 'Madam, my first duchess was a Percy, and she never took such a liberty.'

Jasper Griffin, *Snobs*, 1982

* * *

An Oxford professor of eastern religions was said to have murmured, in an ecstasy of royalism, 'The nicest emperor I know is Germany.'

Ibid.

* * *

When King George V was to lunch at Balliol in Oxford, the menu was sent by the master of the college to the royal household. The menu read, 'Soup, fish, meat, etc.' It was returned with the word 'soup' crossed out and the comment 'No gentleman takes soup at luncheon,' in the margin.

★ ★ ★

An Irish writer, annoyed by Yeats's increased attachment to grand Irish families, complained, 'Yeats is becoming so aristocratic, he's evicting imaginary tenants.'

★ ★ ★

Fritz Kreisler the violinist was asked by Mrs Vanderbilt how much he would charge to play at a private soirée. She was taken aback when he asked for five thousand pounds – a vast sum in the 1930s. She agreed reluctantly, but added, 'Please remember that I do not expect you to mingle with the guests.' 'In that case, madam,' Kreisler replied, 'my fee will only be two thousand.'

# It Takes All Sorts

*(People)*

Field Marshal Montgomery never ceased to patronize his subordinates, among them General Sir Brian Horrocks, 30th Army Corps Commander and Black Rod. Staying with Horrocks and his wife after the war, he insisted on showing them how to pack a suitcase with ease and efficiency. They were much impressed. The lecture at an end, Monty said goodbye and was driven away with his perfectly packed case. An hour later Monty's ADC returned. 'Unfortunately,' he said, 'the Field Marshal left all his shirts behind.'

Quoted in Philip Warner's biography *Horrocks*

\* \* \*

The austerity of his diet was matched by the nudity of his rooms at Cambridge – a table and chair for himself, deckchairs for guests. Wittgenstein would rush from his seminars 'in a state of nervous exhaustion' to see Carmen Miranda or Betty Hutton at the cinema. He preferred American detective magazines to the great journal *Mind*. Bertrand Russell tells the following story about him:

> He used to come to my rooms at midnight and for hours he would walk backwards and forwards like a caged tiger. On arrival, he would announce that when he left my rooms he would commit suicide, so, in spite of getting sleepy, I did not like to turn him out. On one such evening after an hour or two of dead silence, I said to him, 'Wittgenstein, are you thinking about logic or about your

Bertrand Russell

sins?' 'Both,' he said, and then reverted to silence.

Anthony Burgess, reviewing *Wittgenstein* by A J Ayer, *Observer*, 2.6.85

★ ★ ★

'I have the feeling of being a sky-writer who can't spell.'

Robert Benchley, feeling self-conscious in a white suit

★ ★ ★

'You may chalk my figure on your barn door and fire at it. If you hit it, I will know that I should have been hit by you if I had been in the same position.'

William Cobbett when challenged to a duel.

★ ★ ★

Bertrand Russell tells of Ludwig Wittgenstein presenting himself in 1911 on Russell's doorstep in Cambridge. 'Will you please tell me whether I am a complete idiot or not,' said Wittgenstein.

'My dear fellow, I don't know. Why are you asking me?' queried Russell.

'Because if I am a complete idiot I shall become an aeronaut; but, if not, I shall become a philosopher.'

Told by Alan Ryan, *The Times*, 22.4.89

★ ★ ★

A J Ayer the philosopher was shopping with his third wife, Vanessa. When the checkout girl in the supermarket asked him to make out his cheque to 'Marks and Spencer', Ayer asked, 'Is that Spencer as in the poet [Spenser], or the social philosopher [Spencer]?'

I am not sure whether he comes very well out of that story.

Mandrake, *Sunday Telegraph*, 2.7.89

★ ★ ★

The Right Honourable David Wittering memos his private secretary concerning some unresolved business: 'All here has changed. And yet there still seems to be some sense in which it would be true to say that absolutely nothing has changed. All, then, is the same as it was, and yet, simultaneously, nothing like it was whatsoever. At all. What once was true of then, is even more true of now than it was then. If not more so. Or, certainly, less. Would you like a cup of tea?'

\* \* \*

When William Goldman, screenwriter, is not writing, he still goes to his New York office, five days a week. He's been sitting in an office on his own for nearly forty years. 'I'm thrilled when the phone rings. I love it. Even when it's a wrong number.'

Robert Butler, *Independent Review*, 8.11.92

\* \* \*

When things seem to be at their very worst, something too bloody awful is bound to happen.

Daniel George

\* \* \*

An optimist says his glass is half full; a pessimist says it's half empty.

\* \* \*

The optimist proclaims that we live in the best of all possible worlds, and the pessimist fears this is true.

\* \* \*

A pessimist thinks all women are bad; an optimist hopes they are.

Chaucery Depew, Rosten's *Infinite Riches*

\* \* \*

A pessimist is a well informed optimist.

Hungarian proverb

\* \* \*

A medieval courtier incurs his monarch's wrath and faces execution. Begging for mercy he promises that if his life is spared he will have taught the king's favourite horse to speak before a year has passed. The monarch agrees.

Asked why he had made such a crazy promise, the courtier replied: 'Well, the horse might die. Or the king might die. Or the horse might speak.'

*Sunday Express*, 10.6.89, page 33

\* \* \*

There are three ways to ruin yourself: gambling, women and technology. Gambling is the fastest. Women are the most pleasurable. Technology is the most certain.

President Pompidou of France, *Financial Times*, 12.4.88

\* \* \*

Linda Smith, comic at Edinburgh Festival, describes herself as a dyslexic satanist: 'I worship the drivel.'

Observer, *Financial Times*, 1.9.94

\* \* \*

Randolph Churchill, the controversial son of Winston, was operated on for a tumour on his lung. The growth was diagnosed as non-malignant. Said Evelyn Waugh: 'It is a typical triumph of modern medicine that it should find the only non-malignant part of Randolph's body and remove it.'

* * *

Of Macauley, Sydney Smith (1771–1845) said: 'His occasional flashes of silence make his conversation perfectly delightful'.
*Daily Telegraph*, June 1994

* * *

Only one man in a thousand is a real bore – and he is interesting because he is one man in a thousand.
Harold Nicolson, quoted in *Daily Mail*, 8.8.83, page 6

* * *

There was a racehorse once called Hill House that won the Schweppes Gold Trophy at Newbury and by so doing got its trainer, Captain Ryan Price, into all sorts of trouble. It was alleged that he had doped the horse, but some time later he was exonerated when it was discovered that the horse actually manufactured its own cortisone. My recent visit to the Coach and Horses leads me to believe that crashing bores possibly manufacture their own Valium. A glance at them and an earful of them makes me think I should have stayed at home with the cleaning woman, sipping tea while watching her wash the kitchen floor.
Jeffrey Bernard, *Spectator*, 28.4.90

* * *

It is widely believed that John Julius Norwich used actually to cover his eyes with his hands when being driven around London by his mother Lady Diana Cooper. On the final occasion, after she had demolished several traffic lights, he felt the urge to speak. 'Mother, I can no longer bear this.' 'Bear what, dear?' 'Mother, your driving.' 'Am I dear? I thought you were.'

Sheridan Morley, Diary, *The Times*, 25.2.88

\* \* \*

After twenty minutes waiting for a train on the Docklands Light Railway yesterday, one passenger confronted an official. When the official seemed surprised at the accusation, the passenger pointed at the people standing four-deep on the platform and asked: 'If there hasn't been a delay, why are all those passengers still there?' To which the official replied: 'They are not passengers, they are tourists.'

Meanwhile, I wonder what passengers are called in South Africa. *Railway Gazette International* reports the results of a campaign against on-train crime. 'Improved door locks and hopper windows prevent thugs from throwing passengers from the train.'

*Independent*

# Chroniclers of Our Time

*(Press and Journalists)*

Lord Northcliffe wanted to fire an editor and decided to make it easier by first sending him on a world cruise. He offered the job to the deputy editor who turned it down. Efforts to find another editor proved unsuccessful and three months later Northcliffe was reminded that the editor was returning to England. He hurried down to Southampton to meet the ship. As it edged in, the editor saw Northcliffe and waved to his proprietor who was shouting something to him through cupped hands. The editor leaned forward on the ship's rail to hear what Northcliffe was shouting. 'Go round again!' was what he heard.

Told by Derek Jameson on *TV-am*, September 1985

\* \* \*

At times like this I feel rather like the unhappy journalist who went into El Vino's in Fleet Street. Approaching the late Philip Hope-Wallace, he cried: 'Sympathy, sympathy, where can I find sympathy?'

Hope-Wallace looked up briefly from his paper: 'After "shit" but before "syphilis".'

Diary, *The Times*, 7.10.95

\* \* \*

The trouble with the journalist is that he has to work as hard as a millionaire while he hates work as heartily as a mystic. It is a dangerous trade to be at once lazy and busy.

G K Chesterton, quoted in a book review, *The Times*, 31.7.86

\* \* \*

The cardinal sin for a press secretary is to try to cover up a mistake. I was never asked by any minister in any of the administrations I served to distort facts or slant stories...the only exception I can recall occurred one Saturday evening. I was asked to tell an important group of people who had come to meet the prime minister that Mr Callaghan was occupied and would be a few minutes late. I knew that he was determined to watch the end of *The Muppet Show* on television. I complied.

Sir Tom McCaffrey, former Downing Street press secretary, *Daily Telegraph*, 31.7.86, page 16

\* \* \*

To avoid the rigorous press censorship in Russia during Stalin's regime, newspapermen used to devise means of getting their stories through the censor's nets. For the big stories, like the death of Stalin, codes had been prearranged with the news desks back in the West. The wily service reporter had told his desk before leaving London that if they received a cable from him saying 'Please send pounds Sterling 45 in expenses' that meant Stalin was dead but the censor would not let them say so. Having sent the cable, he went home to listen to the BBC short wave expecting to hear himself credited with the scoop of the year. Nothing happened, except that three weeks later £45 appeared in his bank account.

Martin Walker, *Guardian*, 24.3.86

\* \* \*

File in photographic library of *Daily Express* has its contents on the cover classified as:

Shakespeare
William
Playwright
Dead

Milton Shulman, 19.8.87

\* \* \*

An editor is a person, employed on a newspaper, whose business it is to separate the wheat from the chaff and to see that the chaff is printed.

Albert Hubbard

★ ★ ★

Moskowitz, star reporter of a New York Yiddish newspaper, rushed into the press room shouting: 'I've got a scoop! Hold the back page!'

★ ★ ★

Frank Owen was a Fleet Street editor who managed in a short period in the 1950s to get himself fired from a series of editorial posts. Each time he was dismissed he succeeded in getting a lucrative pay-off for loss of office and quickly found himself another highly paid job. Hannen Swaffer, a Fleet Street columnist, commented: 'Frank was born with a silver knife in his back.'

★ ★ ★

Summoning the most basilisk stare I could muster, I once began a talk to a group of budding naval staff officers with the words: 'Gentlemen, I have been asked to talk to you. Not only do I dislike the navy, but I dislike those who serve in it.' The result was pleasing. The audience froze and gazed at me with every evidence of horror and distaste. I then told them that on a recent NATO exercise, the C-in-C Portsmouth, Admiral Sir Arthur Power, had addressed the assembled journalists with the words: 'Gentlemen, I have been asked to welcome you. Not only do I dislike newspapers but I dislike those who write for them.' I was simply testing, I explained, how they would like to be treated as the journalists had been by the admiral. After that they listened to what I had to say.

Charles Wintour, former editor of the *Evening Standard*, discussing the way the navy had treated journalists during the Falklands Campaign, *Observer*, 1.8.82

★ ★ ★

Academics are merely reviewers delivering their copy a hundred years late.

Julian Barnes in *Metroland*, quoted by Christopher Hawtree in *Literary Review*, September 1982

\* \* \*

When Arthur Brisbane was about to complete fifty years of journalism, William Randolph Hearst, his publisher, urged him to take a six month vacation with full pay. This generous offer Brisbane refused to accept, giving two reasons for his doing so. 'The first reason,' he said, 'is that if I stop writing my column for six months it might affect the circulation of your newspapers. The second reason is that it might not affect the circulation.'

Bennett Cerf, *Try and Stop Me*

\* \* \*

Journalism largely consists in saying, 'Lord Jones dead,' to people who never knew Lord Jones was alive.

Quoted from 'The Purple Wig' in *The Wisdom of Father Brown*, by G K Chesterton,

\* \* \*

Newspapers attract nutters likes dustbins attract beagles. No sooner has the cub reporter had his first piece published over his by-line than strange women are telephoning him from Dublin to harangue him about the Blood of the Lamb; complete strangers are trying to sell him life insurance; and men with a faraway look in their eyes are explaining their theories about the authorship of Shakespeare, without pausing to draw breath or allow him to say, 'Er, yes, but . . .'

Philip Howard, *The Times*, 18.3.83

\* \* \*

Prose is words in their best order; poetry is the best words in the best order; journalism is noisy words written in a hurry in any old order.

Philip Howard, *The Times*, 2.9.83

\* \* \*

In the days before screens took over, Reuters had a Wall Street reporter who kept forgetting to put the currency conversions into his stories. So he was demoted to social correspondent.

He went to cover a party and wrote:'Marilyn Monroe came in looking like a million dollars (£317,000 7s 6d.)'

*Financial Times*, 25.1.88

\* \* \*

The London *Times* used to run a regular leader on Saturdays on ecclesiastical topics. Bishops and senior clergymen were usually closeted in a quiet room in the *Times* building to write these religious reflections. The custom was to provide them with a bottle of port to aid them in their reflections. One Friday the copy was getting late and one of the sub-editors gently opened the door of the quiet sanctum to see how the bishop who was writing the editorial was getting on. The bishop was fast asleep, head on the table, the bottle of port was empty and on the sheet of paper in front of the sleeping reverend was the one word 'Notwithstanding...'

\* \* \*

A Salvation Army girl came to a young man sitting alone at a political conference. 'Are you saved?' she asked. 'Press,' he said. 'Oh, I beg your pardon,' she said, and moved hastily away.

A S Neil, Supplement to *Oxford English Dictionary* under 'Press', 1973

\* \* \*

When Alan Watkins, the political correspondent of the *Sunday Express*, had turned in a column to his editor, John Junor, he was met by an enthusiastic editor holding the column in his hand. 'Alan,' said Junor, 'there is only one word to say about this piece... Brilliant! If I were going to print it, I wouldn't change a single comma in it.'

* * *

Quotes always have to be tidied up, because the written word is different from the spoken. Spoken English is full of ums and ers and other little fillers, repetitions, false starts, catachresis and incoherence that would look terrible in print. But good reporters take pains to get their quotes right, and to give a fair representation of what has been said...

The reporter is paid to exercise that mystical faculty, news sense. If he is not good at it, he ceases to be a reporter. As a cub reporter, Mark Twain was instructed never to state as a fact anything that he could not personally verify. Following his instructions to the letter, he filed the following report for the social page: 'A woman giving the name of Mrs James Jones, who is reported to be one of the society leaders of the city, is said to have given what purported to be a party yesterday to a number of alleged ladies. The hostess claims to be the wife of a reputed attorney.'

Philip Howard, *The Times*, 22.6.87

* * *

Called in to discuss future work for the London *Evening Standard*, freelance journalist, Stan Gebler Davis told the editor, John Leese, that he was dying. 'I have terminal cancer and doctors tell me I will soon be dead.' Leese, after a long silence, said, 'Would you like to do a piece about it for the paper?' Gebler Davis, after thinking about it, said, 'Yes, I would, but I want to be paid in advance.' The article duly appeared in the

*Standard* on Monday, 29 February 1988. (And moving it was, too.)

* * *

Even the most celebrated of writers found it something of an ordeal to contribute to the *New Yorker* under William Shawn. That legendary editor, whose retirement was announced last week in his eightieth year, was relentless in checking every fact, every allusion, every intricacy of syntax.

When Alistair Cooke wrote for the magazine about the last days of Edward VIII's reign, Shawn challenged his assertion that the Crystal Palace fire had started at twilight. 'On 30 November 1936,' came the reproof from the *New Yorker*, 'twilight fell ninety minutes after the first fire alarm.'

In 1984, Cooke contributed a long review to the magazine of a book I had written. He proposed calling it, he told me, 'The Resurrection of King George V', but doubted whether the figurative use of the word would pass Shawn's scrutiny.

The editor must have been nodding that week. It did.

Albany, *Sunday Telegraph*, 18.1.87

* * *

Never believe anything until it is officially denied.
Claud Cockburn

* * *

Christopher Hitchens's journalism gives the same good value, mixing jaunty spectacle with tough – and enviably well-informed – political thinking. He has the manner of a lazy Balliol dandy with the killer-instinct of a pit bull terrier. His sour-sweet style is nicely caught in this opening sentence of a piece on John F. Kennedy (at the time of the Cuba crisis)– 'Like everyone else of my generation, I can remember exactly where I was standing and what I was doing on the day President John Fitzgerald Kennedy nearly killed me...' – which elegantly turns a cliché inside-out, says something that you instantly recognize as true, and is calculated to shock the susceptible. Or, 'To listen even very briefly to Ronald Reagan is to realize that here is a man upon whose synapses the termites have dined long and well...'

Review by Jonathan Rabin of *Prepared for the Worst* by Christopher Hitchens, *Observer*, 30.4.89

★ ★ ★

For years after the end of the Second World War, British newspapers were still severely rationed about their use of newsprint. The *Manchester Guardian* was reduced to three editions of eight pages each and three of six pages. Alistair Cooke, their American reporter, cabled the editor that the journalist H L Mencken, had just had a massive stroke and was soon to die. Did the *Guardian* want an obituary? The cabled reply read: 'If dies Monday, Wednesday, Friday, yes. If other days, no.'

★ ★ ★

Back at the Hotel Crillon this evening many anecdotes will doubtless be swapped about Sam White – or 'Amyas Mockbar', as Nancy Mitford portrayed him in *Don't Tell Alfred* – *doyen* of Paris correspondents. My favourite concerns his expenses, which for many years featured the intriguing item 'Flowers for Baroness X' – he justified the pseudonym on chivalrous grounds. When his Fleet Street masters finally sent the message THAT'S ENOUGH BARONESS X STOP, the wily scribe sent in a final claim for 'Flowers for the funeral of Baroness X'.

Peterborough, *Daily Telegraph*, 16.5.91

★ ★ ★

To the extent that a reporter is a Liberal reporter or a Communist reporter or a Republican reporter, he is no reporter at all.

H L Mencken, told to Alistair Cooke in *Six Men* (Penguin)

★ ★ ★

Malcolm Muggeridge used to invite people to lunch without actually remembering who they were. His wife, Kitty, used to enquire in the morning who might be coming for lunch that day. On one occasion Malcolm replied that he thought he had invited 'one of those head-shrinking chappies.' Kitty immediately replied, 'In that case, we had better have Freud fish and Jung potatoes.'

Obituary of Kitty Muggeridge, *The Times*, 14.6.94

★ ★ ★

Kitty Muggeridge said of the TV personality David Frost: 'He rose without trace.'

Ibid.

★ ★ ★

He was saved by the unblinking honesty with which he regarded the wreck of his life, and by his talent for transmuting dishonour into laughter. His readers in following the litany of disenchantment found themselves marvellously released from the burden of ideals.

Obituary of Jeffrey Bernard, 'Low Life' columnist of the *Spectator*, *The Times*, 8.9.97

★ ★ ★

When in 1948, Jeffrey Bernard was asked to leave Pangbourne Nautical College for gambling on horses, the captain of the

college wrote to his mother: 'Dear Mrs Bernard, while I believe Jeffrey to be psychologically unsuitable for public school life, I believe he has a great future as a seam bowler.'
Ibid.

★ ★ ★

For Jeffrey Bernard, the years passed increasingly as an alcoholic blur, so that when he was commissioned to write an autobiography, he had to place an advertisement asking if anyone could tell him what he had been doing between 1960 and 1974.
Ibid.

★ ★ ★

Sir – In order to be taken on the permanent staff of *The Times* in 1954 I was sent for a medical check-up to the firm's doctor. The eye test consisted of being told to look out of the window and asked, 'What is the colour of that London bus?' I got the job and spent thirty-four happy years at Printing House Square.

> Yours faithfully, V E Barnard, (member, *The Times* Night Composing Room, 1954–88), Hatfield, Herts.

Letter to *The Times*, 23.9.97

★ ★ ★

It used to be said that the archetypal *New Statesman* letter-to-the editor in the thirties came under the heading, 'Homosexual offences in the mandated territories'.
Paul Johnson, *Spectator*, 31.7.82

★ ★ ★

When Osbert Lancaster, cartoonist, was asked after he had

175

completed some opera sets for Glyndebourne how stage design compared with pocket cartoons, he replied: 'Bigger. Definitely bigger.'

Review by Godfrey Hodgson of *Osbert*, *Independent*, 8.8.89

\* \* \*

Hugh Cudlipp, editor of *Daily Mirror*, fired his paper's astrologer.

'I wasn't expecting that,' said the surprised astrologer.

'That's *why* you've been fired,' said Cudlipp.

\* \* \*

Back in June 1950 during the North Korean crisis I went out to buy the morning papers and was told all were sold out. The woman behind the counter didn't know why. I said, 'It's because of the danger of war with Russia.' She said, 'It's curious what will sell papers, isn't it?'

Milton Shulman

\* \* \*

FROM RAJ TO RICHES

Headline about art treasures of India, *Independent on Sunday*, 18.10.92

\* \* \*

A headline in a thirties edition of the *New York Times* dealt with an account of a man who escaped from an asylum one night, broke into a laundry, raped two of the workers and ran off. The headline ran: NUT SCREWS WASHERS AND BOLTS.

Centipede, *Guardian*, 22.9.94

\* \* \*

In 1967, Charles de Gaulle made an impassioned speech in

Montreal trumpeting 'Vive le Quebec Libre' and urged a yes vote for a referendum for a separatist Quebec. When he returned to France before the vote, the *Evening Standard* headline ran: OUI, OUI, OUI, ALL THE WAY HOME.

Centipede, *Guardian*, 22.9.94

\* \* \*

After firing William Hardcastle in 1963 and appointing Mike Randall as editor of the *Daily Mail*, Esmond Rothermere told a friend over lunch at the Beefsteak Club why he had switched editors: 'I tried a short fat one and that didn't work. So now I'm having a long thin one.'

Brian MacArthur, *The Times*, 31.7.98

\* \* \*

What exactly *was* Diana, the artiste formerly known as Princess? During her anorexic period, she and Karen Carpenter were the only two famous people whose pictures could fit on to the spine of a CD cover...but St Squidgy, Our Lady of Versace, never sang. She and Mother Teresa were the original ho-spice girls...but Diana never healed anyone. In truth, she was nothing more than a brood-mare crossed with a clothes horse, picked to produce thorough-bred offspring and keep her gob shut in return for occasional 24-carat sugar lumps, and on her tombstone should be written this: Some are born great. Some achieve greatness. And some hire great PR companies.

I wrote the above lines a week after Diana died, intending to include them in a review of that funeral. But they never appeared in print, not because of censorship by the *Evening Standard* but because of a much more insidious form of suppression: self-censorship. Yes, I was one of the many cowardly journalists in desperate need of a spine transplant during the first days of September; but at least I had enough sense of self-preservation to write nothing at all about her, thereby sparing me the ignominy of being quoted on last night's deliciously clinical autopsy of that shameful, frenzied, media-led period, *Diana: The Mourning After* (Channel 4).

Victor Lewis-Smith, *Evening Standard*, 28.8.98

# The Human Enigma

*(Profundities and Pensées, Science, Psychology and Dreams)*

The glass is falling hour by hour, the glass will fall forever,
But if you break the bloody glass you won't hold up the
weather.
Archibald MacNiece

\* \* \*

Confessions may be good for the soul, but they're bad for the
reputation.
Thomas Dewar

\* \* \*

There are ideas that feast on shadow in the prevailing absence
of substance.
William James

\* \* \*

A developer is somebody who wants to build a cabin in the
woods; an environmentalist is somebody who already has a
cabin there.
*Life* Magazine, quoted in *Financial Times*, 5.9.83, page 12

\* \* \*

Maynard Keynes asked his wife, Lydia, what she was thinking
about. 'Nothing,' said Lydia. 'I wish I could,' said Keynes.
Book review by Ronald Blythe in the *Listener*, 29.9.83, page 28

Everyone is a reactionary on subjects he knows about.
Robert Conquest (Kremlinologist), quoted by George Gale, *Daily Express*,
30.12.83

★ ★ ★

Life is not a series of problems. It is a network of mysteries.
Gabriel Marcel (French philosopher), quoted in *The Times*, 31.12.83

★ ★ ★

If one wishes to make a success of life, it is necessary to string
the bow of ambition with the single gut of concentration.
Harold Nicolson

★ ★ ★

How do you know you've forgotten it, when you can't
remember it?'
Alan Bennett, *A Visit From Miss Prothero*, BBC2, 11.1.78

★ ★ ★

Charlie Brown says, 'We are here on earth in order to help
other people.' Lucy thinks about this for a while and asks:
'What are the other people here for then?'
Charles Schulz (cartoonist)

★ ★ ★

The human race is the only species that has a sense of the
ridiculous, can worship its own image and have doubts.

★ ★ ★

Hypocrisy is homage paid by vice to virtue.
La Rochefoucauld

★ ★ ★

Memory is also an art form.
Enoch Powell, *Daily Telegraph*, 23.9.89

* * *

One should try everything once except incest and country dancing.
Arthur Bax

* * *

The writer Primo Levi, answering the question 'How can the Nazis' fanatical hatred of the Jews be explained?' wrote:

> Perhaps one cannot, what is more one must not, understand what happened, because to understand is almost to justify. Let me explain: 'Understanding' a proposal or human behaviour means to 'contain' it, contain its author, put oneself in his place, identify with him; now no normal human being will ever be able to identify with Hitler, Himmler, Goebbels, Eichmann and endless others. This dismays us, and at the same time gives us a sense of relief, because perhaps it is desirable that their words (and also, unfortunately, their deeds) cannot be comprehensible to us.

Review of *The Reader* by Bernard Schlinks, *Sunday Times*, 23.11.97

* * *

When Robert Robinson was asked how you recognize a good conversationalist, he said by the way people cross the road to avoid him.
From *Skip All That*, the memoirs of Robert Robinson

* * *

T S Eliot

The two validating wonders of mortal existence are love and the invention of the future tense.

George Steiner, *Errata: An Examined Life* (1997)

★ ★ ★

Teach us to care and not to care. Teach us to sit still.

T S Eliot

★ ★ ★

For a man to be recognized by posterity though neglected during his lifetime is for insult to be added to injury.

Carlyle

★ ★ ★

> My candle burns at both ends;
> It will not last the night;
> But, ah, my foes, and, oh, my friends –
> It gives a lovely light!

Edna St Vincent Millay

★ ★ ★

The definition of Free Will is doing gladly what I must do.

Jung

★ ★ ★

If you want the truth, invent it.

Line from Pirandello's unfinished play, *The Mountain Giants*, reviewed by Michael Billington, *Guardian*, 16.7.93

★ ★ ★

There is nothing so absurd but some philosopher has said it.

Cicero (106–43 BC)

\* \* \*

As you get older it is harder to have heroes – but I guess it is sort of necessary.

Ernest Hemingway to Lillian Ross

\* \* \*

Truth is often signalled by absurdity.

Kierkegaard

\* \* \*

In every field of human endeavour the fools are bound to outnumber everyone else engaged in that activity.

Milton Shulman, at the Garrick, 11.11.94

\* \* \*

What makes God laugh? Man's plans.

\* \* \*

Masochism, I suppose, is also a form of freedom.

Milton Shulman, reviewing

\* \* \*

Let each child have that's in our care
As much neurosis as the child can bear.

W H Auden

\* \* \*

Hush, Hush,
Nobody cares!
Christopher Robin
Has
Fallen
Down
Stairs

J C Morton (Beachcomber), *Now We Are Sick*

★ ★ ★

Whilst queuing in the bank today, I overheard a mother
reprimand her son (who was starting to draw on the blotting
paper) with the words, 'Thomas, don't do that or I'll close your
account.' Is this the ultimate threat?

Yours, etc., Anna Jackson

Letter to *The Times*, 27.7.89

★ ★ ★

An eight-year-old coming home after a school production of
*Hamlet* said: 'It was very good. All the parents had seen it before
but they laughed just the same.'

Told by Heritage Minister Peter Brooke at *Evening Standard* Film Awards,
30.1.94

★ ★ ★

The intelligent man finds almost everything ridiculous, the
sensible man almost nothing.

Goethe

★ ★ ★

A Chinese philosopher dreamt he was a butterfly. When he
woke he pondered on the possibility that instead of being a

Chinaman who dreamt he'd been a butterfly, he might have been a butterfly dreaming he was a Chinaman.

★ ★ ★

The airplane is a sex symbol. It can also be used to fly from Munich to Vienna.

An analyst, quoted by Julian Symons in his review of Leon Edel's *Stuff of Sleep & Dreams*, *Sunday Times*, 19.9.82

★ ★ ★

The trouble with even sincere and sensible statements is that they can deal only in either tautology or lies. 'Chinese women have exquisite legs.' That cannot be true since there have to be exceptions. 'Some Chinese women have exquisite legs.' That is true but it is not worth saying.

Anthony Burgess, *A Man and Music*, *Sunday Times*, 19.9.82

★ ★ ★

A minute's thought would have shown him that it could not be true. But a minute is a long time and thought is difficult.

A E Housman

★ ★ ★

Woe betide the caller when two terribly fashionable New York phenomena – voicemail and psychoanalysis – collide: 'Hello, welcome to the Psychiatric Hotline. If you are obsessive-compulsive, press 1 repeatedly. If you are co-dependent, please ask someone else to press 2. If you have multiple personalities, press 3, 4, 5 and 6. If you are paranoid-delusional, we know who you are and what you want; just stay on the line so we can trace the call. If you are schizophrenic, listen carefully and a little voice will tell you which number to press. If you are

186

manic-depressive, it doesn't matter which number you press —
no one will answer.'

Observer, *Financial Times*, 1.1.97 (April Fool's Day)

\* \* \*

The trouble with dreams, of course, is that other people's are
so boring.
W H Auden

\* \* \*

A playwright dreamt he was at a grand ball and was waltzing
with the most beautiful woman in the company. When the
music stopped and while waiting for the next number to
begin, he was tapped on the shoulder by a well-known critic
with a reputation for great wit who asked his partner for the
next dance and was about to sweep her off. As he did so, the
critic loudly made a caustic, witty remark which was heard by
everyone and set them all laughing, but quick as a flash, the
playwright came back with a riposte far wittier than the
critic's which was received with even greater appreciation by
the other dancers. Discomfited, the critic slunk away leaving
the playwright to dance away with his pretty partner. At this
moment, the playwright awoke and savouring his brilliant
riposte, he leant over to his bedside table and sleepily wrote
down the remark to preserve it for future use. In the morning
he awoke and recalled the dream. He picked up the paper and
studied what he had jotted down the night before. The words
he had written were: 'And the same to you.'

\* \* \*

William James, the American philosopher and psychologist,
dreamt he had discovered the secret of the universe, woke up
and noted it down, went back to sleep and in the morning saw

that he had written on his notepad: 'Higamus hogamous, woman are monogamous; hogamus higamous, men are polygamous.'

Godfrey Smith, *Sunday Times*, 15.3.88

* * *

Scarfe cartoon showing fat man on palm-tree beach saying, 'Lovely weather, everything wonderful... except me.'

* * *

An antique is a thing which has been useless for so long that it is still in pretty good condition.

Martyn Harris, *Daily Telegraph*, 15.1.88

* * *

Two actuaries went duck shooting. One fired his shot about a foot in front of a duck. The other simultaneously fired his shot about a foot behind the duck. As one, they cried: 'We've got it...'

*Financial Times*, 27.5.87

* * *

At a dinner the poet, John Keats, proposed 'Confusion to the memory of Newton!' On being challenged by Wordsworth to give a justification, he went on to explain: 'Because he destroyed the poetry of the rainbow by reducing it to a prism.'

Richard West, *Spectator*, 4.12.82

* * *

Evidence of the fact that people don't understand science and scientists was the experience of Sir John Hill, physicist and

former chairman of the UK Atomic Energy Authority, who once found himself in a crowded train with a party from a local mental hospital. 'Who are you?' asked the nurse checking her party. 'I am chairman of the Atomic Energy Authority,' Sir John replied. 'Ah, yes . . .' said the nurse, adding him to her list as she continued to count her charges, '. . . four, five, six . . .'
Men and Matters, *Financial Times*, 2.9.86

\* \* \*

Gladstone was asked about Michael Faraday's machines for creating electricity – what were they for and what would they do for England. 'I don't know what they will eventually do for England,' said Gladstone, 'but I do know that the government will tax them.'

\* \* \*

Fred Adams, astrophysicist at Michigan University, calculates that there are almost ten trillion years to go before the lights go out. At that time the universe will be dark and black and our planet will long since have turned to cinders. Beyond that lie 'cosmological decades' embracing the Degenerate Era, populated by mysterious, matter-sucking black holes, and, finally, the Dark Era, threatening to be little more than a diffuse and unfriendly sea of electrons, positrons and radiation. Only then, presumably, will *Coronation Street* be struck off the schedules.
Observer, *Financial Times*, 17.1.97

\* \* \*

Psychoanalysis has all the trappings of an institutionalized religion, with Freud as its prophet, a priesthood, congregation, dogma, ritual and eschatology. It even has its own heretics.
Ann Casement (psychoanalyst)

\* \* \*

Of all Sigmund Freud's contributions to popular speech and amateur psychology, the 'Freudian slip' is probably the most enduring. His life's work, now widely challenged, was to present the mind as an arena where the 'conscious' and 'unconscious' were perpetually at war. The 'slip', whether of word or deed, showed the principle in action. According to the theory, a similar conflict could be found in dreams. But dreams were so complex and significant, based as they were on experiences of early life, that they needed expert advice to unravel. This is why generations of Freudian analysts whose business it has been to do the unravelling have prospered. Freudian slips by comparison are plain man's stuff, allowing everyone to be their own psychologist. When Radio 4's *Today* referred recently to the BBC's 'new spanking building' instead of 'spanking new building', listeners responded to the unconscious innuendo with gleeful letters.

Paul Ferris, *Independent*, 13.8.98

\* \* \*

We used to have lots of questions to which there were no answers. Now, with the computer, there are lots of answers to which we haven't thought up the questions.

Peter Ustinov, quoted by Godfrey Smith, *Sunday Times*, July 1998

\* \* \*

There is absolutely nothing special about our corner of the universe, astronomers have discovered. It is average in every particular. This deflating conclusion, based on images taken by the Hubble Space Telescope, finally lays to rest the belief that human beings have a special place in the cosmos. A team led by Dr Simon Goodwin of the University of Sussex says that where we live is the cosmological equivalent of Swindon. It is normal; it is mediocre; it is dull, dull, dull.

The ancients believed that the earth lay at the centre of the universe, with the sun orbiting around it – a misapprehension corrected by Copernicus and Galileo. Today astronomers believe in the 'principle of terrestrial mediocrity', for which Dr Goodwin and colleagues have found new and persuasive evidence. The last traces of pre-Copernican cosmology lingered on in the feeling that even if the earth, sun and solar system were unremarkable, at least they formed part of an unusual galaxy, much larger than those surrounding it.

Dr Goodwin's team has now made a calculation about the sizes of seventeen galaxies, chosen because they are the same spiral shape as the Milky Way. The average size of these galaxies is 92,000 light years across. And the Milky Way is believed to be 87,000 light years across, which puts it squarely in the middle. 'We live in an average galaxy in all respects,' admits Dr Martin Hendry of the University of Glasgow, a co-author.

The only consolation is that if life has evolved in such an unexcitingly typical galaxy as the Milky Way, it has probably evolved in plenty of other dull places, too. One day we may meet such people and exchange photographs of the local Arndale Centre.

Nigel Hawkes, *The Times*, 5.8.98

# They Know Not What They Do

*(Politics and Politicians)*

During a very tense debate, Labour MP Willie Hamilton was accusing Harold Wilson of ratting on his commitment to the Common Market.

'First he is for the Market,' thundered Willie, 'then he is against. This is not the politics of leadership – it is the politics of *coitus interruptus*.'

There was a shocked silence, then an individual voice yelled: 'Withdraw!'

Told by Joe Ashton, Labour MP, in *Can I Count On Your Support* by Robin Corbett MP and Val Hudson (Stanley Paul Ltd, 1986)

\* \* \*

As there is a degree of depravity in mankind which requires a certain degree of circumspection and distrust, so there are other qualities in human nature which justify a certain portion of esteem and confidence. Republican government presupposes the existence of these qualities in a higher degree than any other form.

James Madison, 1788, quoted in *Time*, 27.6.83, page 33

\* \* \*

Lady Astor, a fierce temperance zealot, speaking at a public meeting declared 'I would rather commit adultery than drink a pint of beer.' A voice from the audience shouted back, 'So would I, your ladyship, so would I!'

\* \* \*

Australian MPs may call each other rats and sheep, but not grubs and dingoes. Bermuda similarly bans termites and India cobras. These are some of the unparliamentary terms of endearment cited by Paul Silk, a senior clerk in the Commons, writing in the house magazine. Westminster shuns jackasses, swine, stool-pigeons, rats, pups, dogs, guttersnipe, murderers, hooligans, ruffians and Pharisees. But it is sad to learn that a New Zealand MP was out of order in declaring that a colleague's brains 'could revolve inside a peanut shell for a thousand years without touching the sides'. In South America, Silk reminds us they do things differently. A legislator of an unnamed country who called another a *cabrón* (mother-fucker)was shot dead by his victim, 'to applause from the rest of the chamber'.

Kenneth Rose, *Sunday Times*, 31.3.85

\* \* \*

While lunching at Chartwell during the fifties, Sir John Howard, former chairman of the National Union of Conservative Associations, remarked to Churchill that one of the Soames children was 'the image' of the great man. In reply Churchill growled, 'All babies are supposed to look like me, Mr Howard. At both ends too.'

Peterborough, *Daily Telegraph*, 16.3.84

\* \* \*

Clem Attlee, after he had ceased being prime minister, took Lord and Lady Packenham to dinner at a West End restaurant. The ex-prime minister took Lord Packenham aside and asked if he would mind paying the bill, promising immediate reimbursement – 'Afraid they don't know me here,' explained Attlee.

Frank Longford, *Eleven at No 10* (Harrap)

\* \* \*

Here richly with ridiculous display
The politician's corpse is laid away.
While all of his acquaintances sneered and slanged,
I wept for I had longed to see him hanged.

Hilaire Belloc

\* \* \*

Equality is an ideal to which many people pay lip service, but which they hope will not be achieved in their own lifetime.

Samuel Brittain, *Listener*, 23.9.83

\* \* \*

I have no respect for the passion for equality, which seems to me to be merely idealizing envy.

Oliver Wendell Holmes (US Supreme Court) in an interview with Nigel Lawson, quoted by Terry Coleman in the *Guardian* in September 1983

\* \* \*

That all men are equal is a proposition to which, at ordinary times, no sane individual has ever given his assent.

Aldous Huxley

\* \* \*

British inequality is the secret of the Tory Party; a recognition that inequality is part of Britain's heritage to be defended not on the grounds that inequality is good, but on the grounds that it is British.

Peregrine Worsthorne, *Sunday Telegraph*, 7.11.82

\* \* \*

The Tory Party consists of that vast residue which would be

hard put to it to describe itself as anything at all – the political equivalent of the millions who go down in the army records as C of E, snobs, idlers, millionaires, craftsmen, landladies, colour-sergeants, milliners, jockeys, innkeepers, academicians, men of genius as distinct from men of talent, anyone and everyone who thinks poetry, money-making, love and sport more important than politics, in fact anyone with anything to lose, if only the opportunity to do nothing.

R J White (Cambridge don), quoted by Peregrine Worsthorne, *Sunday Telegraph*, 15.1.84

\* \* \*

Politics is about the systematic organization of hatred.

Henry Adams

\* \* \*

One of the reasons people turn off political speeches is the irritating number of words that no longer mean anything definite at all. They have been debased into mere noise! Bourgeois, intellectual, militant, middle-class, progressive, Liberal, Fascist, chauvinist. They mean whatever you don't like about someone else or their views. Whereas 'the people' means 'the people who agree with me'; 'the workers' in left-wing speech, means 'our side', whether they work or not.

Peter Lewis, *Daily Mail*, 24.7.82

\* \* \*

Which is the largest country in the world? Estonia, because its coastline is in the Baltic, its capital is Moscow and its population is in Siberia.

Christopher Booker, *Sunday Telegraph*, 15.5.83

\* \* \*

It's a continuing curiosity that Mr [Michael] Foot, orator and *littérateur*, has lost his grasp of words. Watching him manage a sentence is like watching a novice blackbird pulling on a worm: there's a complete lack of confidence about where the thing in his mouth will ever end.

Julian Barnes, commenting on TV coverage of the General Election, *Sunday Times*, 22.5.83

\* \* \*

Enoch Powell has one of the finest minds in Britain – until he makes it up.

Leader, *Sunday Telegraph*, 18.9.83

\* \* \*

He has committed every crime that does not require courage.

Benjamin Disraeli of a political opponent, quoted by Taki, *Spectator*, 27.8.83

\* \* \*

By some means yet to be explained, wild roast pigeons will fly into the mouths of the comrades.

Ludwig von Mises, commenting on *The Theories of Nineteenth-Century Utopian Socialists*, quoted by Jack Wiseman (economics professor), *Listener*, 14.10.82

\* \* \*

In the various countries I have visited, from, for example, the US to India to Yugoslavia to Czechoslovakia, I have found my transactions with taxi-drivers taking much the same form: I want efficient service; they want to be well paid (I choose taxi-drivers for no special reason, save that they are a group normally met while travelling). Would they really become

differently motivated in the New Socialist Society? I don't believe it, and would be worried if I did. I believe that I am more likely to reach the airport on time if the driver is motivated by reward than if he is motivated by comradely love.
Jack Wiseman, ibid.

★ ★ ★

Liberalism is a disease whose first symptom is an inability to believe in conspiracies.
Friedrich Wilhelm IV (1795–1861)

★ ★ ★

In politics while there is death there is hope.
Harold Laski

★ ★ ★

To be political adviser to Mrs Thatcher seems as useful an appointment as being purveyor of fine wines and spirits to the Ayatollah Khomeini or Catholic chaplain to Mr Paisley's Democratic Unionist Party. If Mrs Thatcher is famous for anything, it is for not listening to other people's advice.
Auberon Waugh on appointment of the journalist Ferdinand Mount as Mrs Thatcher's political adviser, *Daily Mail*, 8.7.82

★ ★ ★

The superpowers are ganging up on Margaret Thatcher. Eduard Shevardnadze, the Soviet foreign minister, told the following variant on an old story to George Shultz, his American counterpart, at their last meeting.

Mikhail Gorbachev, Ronald Reagan and Margaret Thatcher go to Heaven on the same day. God says to Gorbachev: 'Well

197

done, my son. Come into my house and sit upon my chair.'
He says much the same thing to Reagan, who is equally
receptive, and it just beginning to say it to Thatcher when
she interrupts: 'I'm not your daughter, it's not your house
and you're sitting in my chair.'

Observer, *Financial Times*, 13.6.88

* * *

An empty taxicab drove up and Calvin Coolidge got out.

(Also said of Clement Attlee)

* * *

Winston Churchill watching Stafford Cripps leave a room:
'There, but for the grace of God, goes God.'

* * *

If you've got them by the balls, hearts and minds will follow.

Sign in office of Charles Culson, presidential adviser to Richard Nixon
during the Watergate crisis.

* * *

We call 'sentimental' a policy or theory which attempts to
reconcile contradictions. The sentimental man will equally
abhor crime and its necessary punishment, disorder and an
organized police. He likes to imagine an impossible world of
mutually exclusive things. It makes him comfortable.

Hilaire Belloc, quoted by Colin Welsh, *Spectator*, 4.9.82

* * *

I remember an occasion when John Strachey, Minister of Food,
completed a slim volume of poems. A long-standing cabinet

rule laid down that any minister proposing to publish a book must seek the premier's permission. 'Oh, prime minister,' said Strachey to Clement Attlee, 'I see that under the rules I have to get your permission to publish a book. Well, I have written a small book of poems. There is nothing political or controversial in them. I take it you will agree to my publishing them.'

Clem's reply was, 'Better send them to me.' Though usually Clem would reply to any communication within twenty-four hours, after a fortnight Strachey had not heard from him and telephoned Number 10. He knew the prime minister had been busy, he began, but assumed he could go ahead and publish. 'Can't publish,' was the reply. When Strachey asked the reason, Clem said: 'Don't rhyme, don't scan.'

Sir Harold Wilson reviewing *Attlee* by Kenneth Harris, *Listener*, 28.9.82

★ ★ ★

Nancy Banks-Smith, TV critic of the *Guardian*, asked Labour Prime Minister Clement Attlee to tell her a joke. 'He gave the matter courteous and serious consideration,' wrote Miss Banks-Smith, 'and began what was, I suspect, his only joke: A man at Speaker's Corner was saying "When the Day of Freedom dawns, you will be living in them houses in Park Lane, you will be riding in them Rolls." A voice from the crowd complained, "I don't want to ride in them Rolls." "When the Day of Freedom dawns," said the speaker, "you will do as you are darn well told."'

*Guardian*, 28.11.83, page 12

★ ★ ★

Who sleeps with whom is intrinsically more interesting than who votes for whom.

Malcolm Muggeridge

★ ★ ★

In an aristocratic society you bribe individuals; in a democracy you bribe classes.
William Gladstone

\* \* \*

Inaccuracy is a way of life in this place.
Speaker George Thomas in the Commons, 24.11.82

\* \* \*

Several US presidents endeared themselves to the public through their pastimes: Ike's Golf, Kennedy's touch football, Truman's piano playing. Hoover took to fishing and throwing a medicine ball, though not at the same time. Nixon had no hobbies to speak of unless one counts the knotting of one's ties.
Roger Rosenblatt, *Time*, 6.12.82

\* \* \*

A cause without a face is a cause without a soul.
*The Times*, 14.3.96

\* \* \*

Lord Birkenhead used the lavatory facilities in the marble splendour of the National Liberal Club every day on his way to the House of Commons from the Temple, despite not being a member. At last a member of staff remonstrated, explaining that it was a club. 'Good God,' said Birkenhead, 'is it that too?'
Charles Nevill, *Daily Telegraph*, 22.10.87, page 14

\* \* \*

After five years of *perestroika*, the Russian people began to pray for the return of Stalin. 'Things are worse, Comrade Stalin,' they cried. 'Please come back.'

After many appeals, the sepulchral voice of Stalin was heard. 'No, no,' he said, 'you have desecrated my memory.'

'Please, please!' cried the people. 'The nation needs you.'

Finally Stalin's ghost relented. 'All right,' he promised. 'I'll come back. but remember, this time there'll be no "Mr Nice Guy".'

Political joke making the rounds in May, 1990

\* \* \*

Late in the 1950s a stuffy Conservative MP stalked into the equally stuffy smoking room at the Commons and complained to its occupants: 'Couldn't get across Bridge Street. Policeman wouldn't stop the traffic for me. Damned fellow said he didn't know who I was.'

At this point the octogenarian Sir Winston Churchill roused himself from apparent slumber and roared: 'All right, who *were* you?' His junior colleague retired, humiliated.

Nicholas Comfort, *Daily Telegraph*, 22.7.88

\* \* \*

There are ten thousand stout men ready to die in the streets of London against popery, though they know not whether it be a man or a horse.

Daniel Defoe

\* \* \*

The trouble with free elections is you never know who is going to win.

Heard in Moscow at the time of democracy's arrival in Russia, 3 January 1992

\* \* \*

Primitive democracy was absurd as well as unfair. (Ninety-five per cent of people had no vote.) In the fifth century BC, there was a moderate right-wing Athenian statesman called Aristides, who was nicknamed by the media of the day as 'the Just'. At the polls, an illiterate citizen asked him to mark his vote for him, in favour of banishing Aristides. 'What harm has he ever done you?' asked Aristides indignantly. 'None,' replied the voter. 'I don't even know the fellow. But I am sick of hearing him always called "the Just".' The impulse to kick the rascals out is old, and is the foundations of democracy.

Peter Howard, *The Times*, 18.4.92

\* \* \*

In personal relations I find Enoch Powell unpredictable. I assume he has mostly deeply disapproved of me. But when I published a rather light biographical essay on Baldwin, he wrote a review which was not only friendly but perceptive. Equally, at the Cambridge Union in 1984, after I had been ill for a couple of months, he suddenly launched into a public tribute which was beyond the call of politeness. I was rather moved and thought it an appropriate peg on which to improve relations, for we had previously stalked past each other without acknowledgement in the corridors of the House of Commons. On the next occasion, when I made to speak, he stalked even more rigidly than usual.

Roy Jenkins, former home secretary, reviewing *Lives of Enoch Powell* by Patrick Cosgrave, *Observer*, 30.4.89

\* \* \*

Huey (Kingfish) Long, autocratic governor of Louisiana for many years, said: 'One of these days the people of Louisiana are going to get good government. And they ain't going to like it.'

Christopher Fildes, *Daily Telegraph*, 10.10.92

\* \* \*

In his days as prime minister, Mr Callaghan was fond of telling pressmen the following story of Clement Attlee, as he was when Labour prime minister. One day a newspaper printed a story so vicious that his press secretary felt that he must show it to Attlee in case the great man should stumble upon it by accident and get a shock. The prime minister ruffled through the pages, uttering his characteristic short bark of 'Yep, yep,' and finally handed the paper back with a snort of disgust. 'What's England coming to?'

It was not until some time later that the press secretary discovered that his leader had been reading the cricket scores. Indeed, Attlee scarcely read anything else.

Mandrake, *Sunday Telegraph*, 19.5.91

* * *

Sir – The following electoral process might comfort those who find the British method of arriving at a new prime minister too tortuous.

The election of the Doge of Venice lasted five days, with two stages of the process allotted to each day. Thirty members of the Great Council, exclusive of those under thirty years of age, were selected by lot. Having retired to a separate room, this group of thirty reduced itself by drawing lots to nine men, who then elected forty men by a majority of at least seven votes each.

After electing the forty, the nine returned to the hall of the Great Council with their list of nominees, being careful as they did so not to look at, speak or make a sign to anyone. Once announced, these nominees were checked so that no family clan had more than one representative, a precaution taken at every subsequent stage of the election.

The new group of forty assembled in a separate room and reduced their number by lot to twelve men, who were to elect the next group of twenty-five by at least seven votes apiece; they were forbidden to nominate themselves, but could elect a member of the previous group of forty.

The twenty-five were reduced by lot to nine, who elected forty-five members by the usual majority of seven votes. The forty-five drew lots to select eleven of their number, and the Eleven (the *Undici*) elected the Forty-one (the *Quarantuno*) who then had to elect a Doge by at least twenty-five votes.

For this final process, the *Quarantuno* were closeted in the senatorial apartments and were not allowed to communicate with the outside world until the Doge was elected. However, in 1516 this final stage took twenty-four days and one hundred and four ballots, and members of the *Quarantuno* were seen climbing out of the windows of the Ducal Palace to collect their bribes.

Yours faithfully, Peggy Woodford, London SW4

Letter to *Independent*, 26.11.90, re Tory procedures for choosing between
John Major, Michael Heseltine and Douglas Hurd to succeed Margaret
Thatcher as leader and prime minister

★ ★ ★

The supreme function of statesmanship is to provide against preventable evils. In seeking to do so, it encounters obstacles which are deeply rooted in human nature.

Enoch Powell, opening lines of his 'Tiber foaming with much blood'
speech against immigration in 1968, quoted by Andrew Marr, *Independent*,
20.11.92

★ ★ ★

Henry Kissinger was in London last week for a succession of parties to celebrate his seventieth birthday: breakfast with Bain and Co, the management consultants; lunch with Lord and Lady Weidenfeld; dinner at Spencer House. He related a conversation he had had with Larry Eagleburger, briefly US secretary of state, about the American invasion of Grenada.

'Why did we do it?'

'To see if we could bring democracy to nations of a hundred thousand people.'

'What happens if it goes wrong?'

'We'll try nations of sixty thousand.'

Kenneth Rose, *Sunday Telegraph*, 31.10.93

* * *

Gladstone suffered terribly from sea-sickness. His doctor advised him to try to concentrate on something so interesting that it would take his mind off it. The Grand Old Man's solution was to read a book called *Pickering on Adult Baptism*.

Mandrake, *Sunday Telegraph*, 13.3.94

* * *

The politician who complains about the press is like the ship's captain who complains about the sea.

Enoch Powell

* * *

One junior minister was summoned precipitately to No. 10 Downing Street (the home of British prime ministers) to be congratulated, so he thought, on the work of his department. 'I want your job,' said Clement Attlee. The minister was staggered. 'But, why, prime minister?' 'Afraid you're not up to it,' said Attlee. The interview was over.

Attlee by Kenneth Harris

* * *

As political scandals go it is hardly up there with 'cash for questions', 'arms to Iraq' or the Profumo Affair; but the Tories in Wales are none the less getting mighty exercised about cheese sandwiches. Claims of 'cheese sleaze' have been made after it emerged that Plaid Cymru offered voters a cup of tea and a sandwich at an agricultural show, just days before a local council by-election. Peter Davies, the chairman of South East Wales Conservatives, said the Plaid Cymru candidate, Darren Jones, was guilty of a 'very serious breach of election law'. Mr Davies added, 'If it had just been a cup of tea or coffee we probably wouldn't have done anything but when it comes to sandwiches it is the thin end of the wedge.' Mrs Clem English, who sparked the controversy with a letter of thanks in the local paper, said: 'The sandwiches were very nice but they didn't influence my vote. If the Tories had been offering chocolate cake I would have eaten it but I still wouldn't have voted for them.'

Kate Watson-Smith, *Independent*, 29.8.98

★ ★ ★

My favourite historical parallel is the famous Abraham Lincoln and John F. Kennedy conundrum. Lincoln was elected to Congress in 1846, Kennedy in 1946. Lincoln became president in 1860, Kennedy in 1960. Lincoln's secretary was named Kennedy, Kennedy's was named Lincoln. Both were assassinated on a Friday by Southerners. John Wilkes Booth ran from the theatre and was caught in a warehouse. Lee Harvey Oswald ran from the warehouse and was caught in a theatre. Both Lincoln and Kennedy were succeeded by men named Johnson: Andrew Johnson was born in 1808, and Lyndon Johnson was born in 1908. Finally, both assassins, Booth and Oswald, were killed before their trials. Now that is uncanny.

Amanda Foreman, *Spectator*, 16.5.98

# How Old is God?

## (Religion)

Lady Cunard suddenly turned to Ribbentrop and said, 'Tell me, Mr Ambassador, what does your Fuhrer think about God?' There was a sort of dead silence and everyone sat on the edge of their chairs wondering what was going to happen next and Ribbentrop seemed as much embarrassed as everyone else, and eventually said, 'He has not yet quite decided.'

John Julius Norwich, recounting a 1937 lunch for Hitler's ambassador, attended by his mother. *Trans-Atlantic Quiz*, reported in *Listener*, 14.10.82

★ ★ ★

When you speak to God it's called praying; but when God speaks to you it's called schizophrenia.

Cynical journalist at trial of Peter Sutcliffe, the 'Yorkshire Ripper'

★ ★ ★

The exacting of an eye for an eye only leads to a lot of blindness.

Gita Mehta, *Spectator*, 4.12.82

★ ★ ★

On a Welsh chapel poster announcing 'The Meek Shall Inherit the Earth', someone had written, 'Serve them right.'

*Financial Times*, 30.8.83, page 12

★ ★ ★

The mumbo-jumbo of ecology is another substitute for religion. Indeed it is a kind of religion, a modern form of paganism. It teaches us to worship stones. It deifies animals, rather as the ancient Egyptians made gods out of cats, crocodiles, monkeys and ibexes, mummifying them in colossal numbers. It puts 'wilderness areas' before people.

Paul Johnson, *Daily Telegraph*, 22.1.83

★ ★ ★

A young woman in a museum asked a curator to identify a stuffed bird. 'It's a guillemot,' she was told. 'That's not my idea of a guillemot,' said the young woman. 'It's God's idea of a guillemot,' said the curator.

★ ★ ★

If God were suddenly condemned to live the life which He has inflicted on men, He would kill Himself.

Alexander Dumas *fils*, from *Gross's Aphorisms*

★ ★ ★

A religion which becomes Perhaps will not stand in the day of battle.

John Buchan on Calvinism

★ ★ ★

A Welsh sea captain was shipwrecked on a Pacific island and several years later he was discovered by a passing frigate. 'How long have you been here?' asked the naval officer who came ashore to rescue him. 'Fifteen years,' replied the Welshman. 'Didn't you get bored?' asked the officer. 'At first I did,' said the Welshman, 'but then I set my hands to God's service.' He took the naval officer through a belt of trees and in a small valley stood two stone chapels. 'Good heavens!' said the officer. 'Did you build those with your own hands?' The Welshman nodded. 'But why two? Wasn't one sufficient for your devotions?' 'Ah, you see,' said the Welshman pointing to the farther chapel, 'that's the one I don't go to.'

★ ★ ★

Just at this very moment in human destiny, when the Devil has shown himself at his wiliest and most clear-sighted, the churches blindfold themselves afresh into a condition of pristine gullibility, as if they had never heard the bad news about the Fall of Man.

Peregrine Worsthorne, *Sunday Telegraph*, 8.8.82

★ ★ ★

An honest God is the noblest work of man.

Robert Ingersoll

★ ★ ★

An atheist is a man who has no invisible means of support.

John Buchan

★ ★ ★

In C S Lewis's *Screwtape Letters*, the senior devil instructs his apprentice to direct his victim's decent instincts towards mankind as a whole, and his selfishness, vanity and cruelty towards those around him. In that way, the decency will be largely theoretical and the viciousness only too real.

John O'Sullivan, editor of *US Policy Review*, *Daily Telegraph*, 20.9.82

★ ★ ★

A lecturer on religion told his audience 'that the world would probably end in seven billion years.' 'How long did you say?' came an anxious voice from the rear of the audience. 'Seven billion years,' the lecturer repeated, firmly. 'Thank God,' said the voice, 'I thought for a moment you had said seven *million*.'
Bennett Cerf, *Try and Stop Me*, page 134

\* \* \*

Many people genuinely do not wish to be saints, and it is probably that some who achieve or aspire to sainthood have never felt much temptation to be human beings.
George Orwell

\* \* \*

A mouse is enough to stagger sextillions of infidels.
Walt Whitman

\* \* \*

It is noticeable that in all this discussion about the femininity of God, the masculinity of the Devil goes unchallenged. This is unfair and revealing!
Christopher Russell in a letter to *The Times*, 28.10.83

\* \* \*

History tends to prove that faith is reborn from its own embers.
Graham Greene, quoted by Malcolm Muggeridge, *Spectator*, 23.4.83, page 20

\* \* \*

A French mathematician observed: 'I do not know as much as God. But I know as much as He did at my age.'

\* \* \*

In his autobiography *The Last Breath*, the film-maker Luis Buñuel tells of seeing a notice on a convent door which read: 'Traveller, if your conscience is troubling you, knock and we shall open. No women.'
*Guardian*, 26.1.84, page 12

\* \* \*

Discussing the proposed ordination of women into the Church of England, Father Ross Thompson, Rector of Cowley, said: 'We're rapidly becoming a Mickey Mouse church. We've always had crazy bishops, quite out of touch with the parishes, but this Synod would abolish God on a two-thirds majority!'
*Sunday Telegraph*, 26.5.85, page 17

\* \* \*

Jews will still have to exist even when the last Jew has been wiped out.
Elias Canetti, Nobel-Prize winning author of *Auto-da-Fé, The Times*, 27.7.85, page 8

\* \* \*

> Forgive, O Lord, my little jokes on Thee
> And I'll forgive Thy great big one on me.

Robert Frost (American poet), quoted by PM Rajiv Gandhi at Lord Mayor's lunch, 15.10.85

\* \* \*

'Curate wanted for country parish, slow left arm bowler preferred.'
Advertisement in personal column of *The Times*

\* \* \*

Printed on the inside cover of a theological work: 'Spread the word of the Lord. No part of this book may be reproduced without permission from the publishers.'
*Financial Times*, 17.5.84, page 26

*  *  *

If reason is a gift of Heaven and the same is to be said about faith, then Heaven has made us two incompatible and contradictory presents.
Diderot, quoted by Alastair Forbes, *Spectator*, 15.9.84, page 29

*  *  *

For the Vatican, the last 'news story' was the life and death of Jesus Christ. The next news story will be Armageddon.
Patrick Marnham, *Spectator*, 10.5.85

*  *  *

Does anyone exist more Catholic than the Devil?
Charles Pierre Baudelaire

*  *  *

God is alive and well but engaged on a more ambitious project.

*  *  *

If God had invented or thought of something better than sex, He would have kept it to Himself.

*  *  *

Heine on his deathbed was being comforted by his wife who said, 'I pray God will forgive you your sins.' 'Of course he will,' said Heine, 'that's his job.'

*  *  *

An Irish Protestant on his deathbed, asked if he would renounce the Pope, the flesh and the Devil, replied 'In my condition, I can't afford to antagonize anyone.'

★ ★ ★

The *New Yorker* said of the Bible: 'You've seen the picture, now read the book.'

★ ★ ★

St Augustine prayed to be virtuous, 'but not yet'.

★ ★ ★

Children had been asked to write their own nativity play and try to give it a modern flavour. Mary, aged eight, is nursing a large doll when Joseph enters. 'Hello, Mary!' he greets her. 'How have you been getting on with baby Jesus?' Mary rocks the holy infant vigorously. 'You may well ask! He's been a right little bugger all day!'

Godfrey Smith, quoting Mencap book *Suffer Little Children, Sunday Times*, 10.5.87

★ ★ ★

Godfrey Winn, journalist and gossip columnist, once said, 'Well, I don't care what anybody else thinks about God. He has always been perfectly sweet to me.'

Arthur Marshall, *Sunday Telegraph*, 12.7.87

★ ★ ★

The American photographer Horst P Horst believes in the afterlife and is sufficiently confident to suppose he will be happy in Heaven – as he said, 'Providing the angels are beautifully attired and wear their halos at a tilt.'

Drusilla Beyfus, *Vogue*, May 1987

Then there are those who see the Subcontinent clothed in two clichés: (a) poverty juxtaposed with immense wealth, the subject of a hundred documentaries and (b) mysticism. Only the sixties' generation sees India primarily as the land of roll-ups and hashish – a gas, man!

The only antidote to these images is irony. So I offer a paraphrase of a short story by Manto: A village is beset by drought, scarcity, riots. The police are searching for hoarders. One small fry hoarder has stored three sacks of sugar for which he knows he will be lynched. He decides to dispose of them and takes them by night to the village well and lowers them in with the help of a rope to avoid the sound of a splash. The rope on the last sack gets tangled in his legs and he's dragged into the well and drowned. The next day his body is found in the well. The day after, his grave is consecrated by the poor village folk as that of a saint – the water of the well has turned sweet!

Farrukh Dhondy, commissioning editor for multicultural programmes at Channel 4, *Listener*, 5.8.87

\* \* \*

If absolute power corrupts absolutely, where does that leave God?

Overheard, Garrick Club, 26.5.91

\* \* \*

*Quest*, the journal of the austere Queen's English Society, this quarter – tight-lipped – provides Ten Black Commandments from the African American Family Press's *The Black Bible Chronicles*:

I am the Almighty, your God who brought you outta Egypt when things were tough. Don't put anyone else before Me.

Don't make any carved objects or things that look like what is heaven or below. And don't bow down to these things like they are anything heavy. Not ever!

You shouldn't diss the Almighty's name, using it in cuss words or rapping with one another. It ain't cool, and payback's a monster.

After you've worked six days, give the seventh to the Almighty.

Give honour to your mom and dad, and you'll live a long time.

Don't waste nobody.

Don't mess around with someone else's ol' man or ol' lady.

You shouldn't be takin' nothing from your homeboys.

Don't go tellin' lies on your homebuddies.

Don't want what you can't have or what your homebuddy has. It ain't cool.

Ruth Dudley Edwards, *Independent*, 24.4.95

★ ★ ★

Perhaps Sir Alfred Ayer the wit occasionally betrayed Sir Alfred Ayer the logician. I remember his saying in a broadcast interview, 'I know that there is not a God in the way I know that there is not a rhinoceros in the room.' Surely one knows that there is not a rhinoceros in the room because one also knows that there is a rhinoceros somewhere.

Miss N M Nicholson, London W5

Letter to *Sunday Times*. 9.7.89

★ ★ ★

An act of God is an act no reasonable man would expect God to commit.

★ ★ ★

When Einstein was asked by a New York rabbi whether he believed in God, he replied that he believed in Spinoza's God, 'who reveals himself in the orderly harmony of all that exists, not in a God who concerns himself with the fates and actions of human beings'.

Ronald Clark's biography of Einstein

\* \* \*

Einstein said time and time again, 'God does not play dice with the universe.'

Jeremy Bernstein's biography of Einstein

\* \* \*

Somerset Maugham once asked the Victorian man of letters Augustus Hare, whose practice it was to read aloud to his household from the *Book of Common Prayer*, why he omitted all passages glorifying God. 'God is a gentleman,' Hare replied, 'and no gentleman cares to be praised to his face.'

Quoted by Laurence Mark, *Observer*, page 21 (in an article re Robert Maxwell)

\* \* \*

The scientist Leo Sziland said he was going to keep a diary, not for publication, but as a record of the facts. For God. When it was suggested that God already knew the facts, he said, 'But he doesn't know *this version* of the facts.'

Katherine Whitehorn, Observer 5.6.94, page 25

\* \* \*

Comedian Paul Merton says he began to reject the tenets of Catholicism well before his teens. 'All those extremes,' he says. 'To be told that there is either eternal bliss, walking around the clouds playing table tennis with Mozart and Cary Grant, or eternal damnation where you have to light Hitler's cigars – it does give you something to kick against.' He continued going to church until he was fifteen to avoid big scenes with his parents.

Simon Garfield, *Guardian*, 29.8.98

\* \* \*

Today I buried my father-in-law at sea. Buried is probably not the word for it. There was no body. What we did was cast his ashes to the four winds. I've never seen a person's ashes before. I suppose I'd unthinkingly assumed that 'ashes' was only a way of speaking, that what we burn down to is some sort of odoriferous powder, finer and sweeter-perfumed than talcum, and somehow still animated by soul. But we don't. We make the same sort of ash as a bonfire makes. Grey and grainy and unspiritual. Plenty of it, too. A whole plastic flaskful, which can take a fair bit of shaking out. Especially if your hands aren't steady.

I've never fancied being burned myself. I'm too worried about the possibility of a mistake. Imagine lying inside that highly flammable wooden lozenge and listening to it crackle while you're still alive, still able to hear the congregation singing 'Jerusalem'. Imagine the condition of your mind. Illogical, I know, given that you can be buried alive just as easily. But then I've never fancied the soil option either. Earth, water, air, fire – let those who were happy to live in the elements, die in the elements. You're either an earth's diurnal course man or you're not. I'm not. I keep hoping I can hold out long enough for someone to discover some new and more suitable medium for my expiry. Something less natural. Evaporation through abstruse sentence, say. Interment in metaphor. Scatter me in words, O my beloved.

Howard Jacobson, *Independent*, 31.8.98

# Sex is an Inexact Science

*(Sex)*

A sociologist doing a study of brothels discovered that one of the prostitutes had a doctorate in oriental studies, spoke five languages fluently, had written two novels and had a father who was a millionaire. 'How did a girl like you get into a place like this?' asked the surprised academic. 'Just luck, I guess,' came the reply.

★ ★ ★

Robert Redford was asked by an interviewer how did it feel to know that he could have any woman in the world. To which he replied, 'Where were they when I needed them?'

★ ★ ★

On his twenty-first birthday a young officer in the Welsh Guards was given the following advice by his father. 'Never hunt south of the Thames, never drink port after champagne and never have your wife in the morning lest something better should turn up during the day.'

Laurence Olivier, in his autobiography, page 145

★ ★ ★

The sexual urge of the camel is greater than anyone thinks
After several months in the desert, it attempted a rape on
  the Sphinx.
Now the intimate parts of that Lady are sunk 'neath the
  sands of the Nile.

Hence the hump on the back of the camel and the Sphinx's inscrutable smile.

Artillery-camp graffito, Cairo 1940, from *Graffiti 3* by Nigel Rees

\* \* \*

The pleasure is momentary. The posture is ridiculous. The expense is damnable.

Lord Chesterfield (1694–1773)

\* \* \*

If I drank as much and had as many women as I have said I have, I would be in a jar in the Massachusetts Institute of Technology.

Frank Sinatra, quoted by Taki, *Daily Telegraph*, 11.6.86, page 3

\* \* \*

Colombo (Reuters) – Men who wore condoms on a finger or took the Pill meant for their wives were two reasons for contraceptives often being ineffective in Asia, a United Nations report said yesterday. The report to the Third Asian and Pacific Population Conference related that remote Asian villagers had been shown how to wear condoms in demonstrations with a bamboo pole. When field workers returned several months later they were confronted by groups of irate pregnant women. Enquiries disclosed that men had been wearing condoms on a finger or keeping them on a bamboo pole. Investigations also discovered that in many instances condoms had been boiled or swallowed. The most common pitfall with the Pill, the report said, was that men were taking it instead of women.

'Why the Pill's success rate is low in Asia', article in *The Times*, 28.9.82

\* \* \*

Sign seen in the rear window of a car being driven by a young man in Chelsea: 'National Sex Week. Please give generously.'

Observer, *Financial Times*, 13.9.88

★ ★ ★

My own belief is that there is hardly anyone whose sexual life, if it were broadcast, would not fill the world at large with surprise and horror.

Somerset Maugham, quoted by Julian Barnes, *Observer*, 24.7.83

★ ★ ★

On the back door in the editorial room [of the *New Statesman*] there hung an old and very dirty macintosh, said to have belonged to H G Wells. Any man who put it on, the legend continued, would sleep with the first woman he met. But nobody tried it out, for fear of meeting one of those fierce, iron-grey Hampstead Socialist ladies who used to visit the *Statesman* to put them right on their policy to Albania.

Richard West, quoted in *Spectator*, 5.6.82, page 32

★ ★ ★

> I may be fast, I may be loose
> I may be easy to seduce.
> I may not be particular
> To keep the perpendicular –
> But all my horizontal friends
> Are princes, peers and reverends.
> When Tom or Dick or Bertie call
> You'll find me strictly vertical.

Herbert Farjeon, quoted in review of the memoirs of Elsa Lanchester, *Sunday Telegraph*, 11.9.83

★ ★ ★

Of a hermaphrodite: 'It was a lousy day. He wasn't feeling herself.'

★ ★ ★

Mae West said she likes to wake up in the morning feeling a new man.

★ ★ ★

A young soldier had sexual relations with a transvestite male dressed as a WRAC major, a court was told yesterday. Gunner Adam Lamb, aged 19, said he was under the influence of alcohol when he was approached by Stuart Wylie, aged 22, as he walked back to his barracks in Colchester, Essex. Gunner Lamb said he was convinced that Mr Wylie, of Leather Grove, Colchester, was a woman. Mr Wylie, who has pleaded not guilty to gross indecency and other sexual offences against three soldiers, was dressed as a woman major.

Mr Wylie's true sexual identity was not revealed during the sexual act, Gunner Lamb told Ipswich Crown Court. He said he first learnt of Mr Wylie's gender some days after the event. 'I had in my mind that it was a major in the WRAC. For most soldiers, that is quite an achievement,' he said. The trial continues today.

*The Times*, 6.1.88

★ ★ ★

Rightly or wrongly, Valery Giscard d'Estaing has long had something of a reputation of a womanizer, and gossip credited him with a very active private life even during his seven-year tenure as president of France. This is teasingly confirmed in his memoirs, extracts of which have appeared in the French press.

'During my *septennal*,' he says, 'I was in love with seventeen million French women ... The word must be taken in its most

**Mae West**

precise sense. I am, of course, aware that this declaration will provoke ironic comments, and that English-speaking readers will find it 'very French'. But it is true that I felt directly the presence of French women in the crowd, I guessed their silhouette, and I lingered just a little longer to look at them, that extra half-second in which there suddenly appears in the eyes the nakedness of existence.' Indeed. How very French!

Observer, *Financial Times*, 26.2.88

\* \* \*

The Prince de Jounville after seeing a performance by the Great Rachel, in the mid 1800s, sent his card to her dressing room with the words: 'Where? – When? – How much?' To which she replied: 'Your place – Tonight – Free.'

Antonia Fraser, *Love Letters*

\* \* \*

The Chelsea Clinical Society was founded in 1897 and is the most prestigious of medical associations. It has a limited membership of three hundred and a five-year waiting list. The great and the good of London medicine have been members over the years. For the past decade, the society has met at the Berkeley Hotel in Knightsbridge. Among the speakers have been Princess Anne, King Hussein of Jordan, Lord Whitelaw, Lord Home and Lady Thatcher.

When Atticus was invited to speak by the secretary, Stanley Rivlin – after a suggestion from my elbow doctor, Keith Bush – he expected a small gathering of an elderly bunch and prepared accordingly. Not for the first time, I got it completely wrong. The banquet room was full, the people dressed in their finest, and the atmosphere festive and irreverent. The wine flowed like Diana's tears.

The acting president, Richard Lavelle, senior surgeon at Bart's, gave me a wonderful introduction. But just as I stood up, in front of hundreds, a nice lady pointed at my trousers and suggested I pull up my zip. In my hurry not to be late, I had left my fly wide open.

Despite the inauspicious start, it was a thoroughly English affair, full of good humour and good manners, and I had some fun. The subject of my speech was how the media often get it wrong. I included the following vignette: a couple of weeks ago, Barbara Walters, the David Dimbleby of Yankee TV, interviewed Neil Armstrong and asked if he had rehearsed his famous line about one small step for man, one giant leap for mankind as he first stepped on the moon?

'Not only didn't I rehearse it, I never said it,' replied the astronaut.

'What did you say, then?' wondered La Walters.

'I said it's a giant leap for Manny Klein.'

'Who is Manny Klein?' wondered La Walters.

'Manny Klein was my room-mate in school,' answered Armstrong, 'and I was best man at his wedding. That night he asked his bride for oral sex and she refused. "Not on your life! Not until a man walks on the moon!"'

One thing is sure. My speech was different from the Princess Royal's and Lady T's.

Taki, *Sunday Times*, 10.12.95

\* \* \*

An anonymous woman said that making love to the large, rotund Nicholas Soames, Minister of Defence (1995) and grandson of Winston Churchill, was 'like having a wardrobe fall on top of you with the key sticking out'.

*Independent*, 3.4.98, page 3

\* \* \*

Fiona MacCarthy's life of Eric Gill uncovers a lot that has not been made public before. It appears from Gill's diaries that he enjoyed incestuous relationships over a long period with two of his sisters and with his two elder daughters. He also had sexual congress with a dog. For a lay brother of the order of St Dominic, who wore the girdle of chastity of the Confraternity of Angelic Warfare, this is obviously not a good record.

John Carey, reviewing *Eric Gill* by Fiona MacCarthy, *Sunday Times*, 22.1.89

\* \* \*

'Of course, this isn't the first case I've come across of a man seeking sexual gratification from his vacuum cleaner,' Public Safety Director Louis Napoletano told reporters in Long Branch, New Jersey, 'but this guy obviously didn't know his model very well. If he had, he'd have known that right under where the hose attaches, there's a revolving blade for pushing the dust into the collection bag.'

Napoletano was speaking the day after a fifty-one-year old man had been rushed to the Monmouth Medical Center with a severed penis and severe blood loss. 'When police officers responded to his 911 call, they burst into his house and found him lying in a pool of blood. At first, he told them that he had cut himself shaving. Then he said someone had broken in and stabbed him in the crotch, but the vacuum cleaner was covered in blood, and one of the officers found the amputated tip of his penis in the dust bag, so it was pretty obvious what had happened.

'We got him to the medical center as soon as possible, and doctors tried to reattach the severed part, but without success. This morning, the man admitted to us that he'd got drunk while his wife was away, and had decided to seek sexual pleasure from the vacuum suction. It just goes to show, you should do what the manufacturers say: always read your appliance handbook before switching it on.'

*Associated Press*, 13.5.98, sent to *Private Eye* by Andy Davison

# Winning is an Addiction
### (Sport and Games)

Groucho Marx was taken to see his first cricket match and sat in rapt attention for half an hour. Finally his host turned and asked him how he was enjoying himself. 'Fine,' said Groucho. 'When does it start?'

Godfrey Smith, *English Companion*, page 72

\* \* \*

Sixteen years ago a gentleman, Colonel Stewart Ramsey by name, asked me in the dressing room whether I would care to organize tennis games. We started playing every Thursday – whenever weather permitted. Indeed, often even when weather did not permit we played – in rain, hail, fog and snow.

Coming off court one day he once remarked he was the only one among us who never cancelled for health reasons, and added 'Not even when I had a stroke.'

By that time I knew Stewart intimately but this was the first time I had heard about a stroke. I knew that he had been a distinguished soldier, a former games manager of Hurlingham, a former running champion of the British army, a man of few words yet a man of the *mot juste*. Yes, I knew quite a lot about him but nothing about a stroke. Later that evening I saw Dorothy, Stewart's elegant wife, so I asked her: what was this talk about a stroke?

For the first time in her life she had left Stewart alone for four days in London. On the first day he had a slight stroke. He decided the best remedy in such cases was to go on playing tennis. And he did. As this happened on a Bank Holiday weekend, he played three times – Saturday, Sunday and Monday. Somehow, perhaps miraculously, he survived.

Stewart came to join us. 'Yes,' he said listening to our conversation, 'It is my ambition to perform a good smash and die on the tennis court.'

His wish was granted in his eighty-fifth year, on a sunny Tuesday afternoon, this April. But not quite. He – a lovable man, a great gentleman and a good friend – died on the tennis court as he wished, but not after a magnificent smash: he died after a double fault. Well, you can't have everything.

George Mikes, *Hurlingham Club News*, August 1985

★ ★ ★

A golfer, teeing off, boasted to his partner about his new and extraordinary golf ball. 'If it goes into the rough, it sends out a radio bleep,' he said. 'When it goes into water it rises to the surface, and it glows in the dark.' 'Amazing,' said his friend, impressed, 'where did you get it?' 'I found it,' said the golfer.

Men and Matters, *Financial Times*, 11.6.84; Diary, *Financial Times*, 13.3.92

★ ★ ★

Willie Papp, a former lightweight boxing champion, was reported to have died. When a sports journalist phoned his home to get some details for an obituary he was surprised to hear Papp's voice on the other end of the line. 'Willie,' said the reporter, 'we'd heard you'd died last night.' 'Died!' answered Papp. 'I didn't even go out last night.'

★ ★ ★

If tonight the Germans beat England at our national game, we have the consolation of knowing that we have twice beaten them at theirs.

Vincent Mulchrome, writing about a coming football game between England and West Germany, quoted by Peter McKay, *Evening Standard*, 30.6.86

★ ★ ★

227

Omar Sharif, actor and bridge player, says that King Farouk of Egypt had an unbeatable way with cards and that no one ever won against him because he would simply put his cards down and say, 'I've won. I have better cards.' The king was once in a game of poker and an opponent had the effrontery to declare that he had three queens. Farouk retorted that he had three kings, and when someone turned up his cards to reveal only two kings, Farouk snarled, 'I'm the third.'

Peterborough, *Daily Telegraph*, 14.8.86

* * *

Sir Osbert Lancaster, designer and cartoonist, after his first few days on the river in his Oxford days at Lincoln, wrote: 'It became abundantly clear to me why rowing had in more rational societies been confined to the criminal classes and prisoners of war.'

Albany, *Sunday Telegraph*, 24.4.88

* * *

I must take issue with your literary editor's claim that 'good at chess means good at little else'. The following people were master standard (or approaching it): Turgenev, Tolstoy, Prokofiev, Marcel Duchamp, David Oistrakh, Alfred de Musset, Andrew Bonar Law, Toto, Karl Marx, Pope Leo XIII, Che Guevara, János Kádár, Jacob Bronowski.

Just below that, but still pretty good were, or are, William Golding, Michael Foot, Yehudi Menuhin, Mendelssohn, Roget, Humphrey Bogart, Ossie Ardiles, Steve Davis, Samuel Becket, Patrick Moore, Aleister Crowley and Alastair Sim.

Ex-world champion Smyslov was a concert-standard baritone. Grandmaster Taimanov is a concert pianist and Karpov is not bad at snooker.

Yours faithfully, Michael B Fox, Edgbaston, Birmingham

Letter to *The Times*, 26.1.88

* * *

Firemen with a weight problem were urged to get fit. When the Home Office issued this directive, a notice went up in the HQ of the Herefordshire Fire Department, saying there was no need for a fitness programme. 'Everyone gets enough exercise jumping to conclusions, passing the buck, flying off the handle, running down the boss, dodging responsibility and pushing their luck.'

*Guardian*, 16.8.86, page 26

\* \* \*

In mathematics you need to be right. In chess you only need to be more right than your opponent.

Dr John Nunn, chess grandmaster, *Guardian*, 21.8.83

\* \* \*

Ocean racing is like standing under a cold shower in a howling gale tearing up ten-pound notes.

Edward Heath, former British prime minister, *The Times*, 21.8.82, page 8

\* \* \*

Louis Freedman, who won last year's Derby and other valuable races with his colt Reference Point, has a two-year-old this season by Habitat out of Guillotina. As yet unproved, it at least bears an appropriate name: Headquarters. That has not exhausted its owner's ingenuity. He has sent his mare Guillotina to be covered by the stallion Legend of France. Why? So that he may call their progeny, due to be born any day now: Eat Cake.

Kenneth Rose, *Sunday Telegraph*, 10.4.88

\* \* \*

Germany has written to me. It wants to know how good my tennis is. It wrote, moreover, beneath the letterhead of the Queen's Club, home of the Lawn Tennis Association: an imprimatur impregnable to scrutiny. It seems that the Fatherland has persuaded the game's governing body to set up something entitled the LTA Volkswagen Ratings Computer, and it is this which invited me to submit my game to software eager to determine my playing status. Those who come up to snuff will doubtless be offered German nationality, in the fervent patriotic hope that this year's Wimbledon Ball may be opened by someone trundling Steffi Graf backwards for the twinned glory of the Bundesrepublik.

Very flattering, of course, but also puzzling. How did Volkswagen know I played tennis? Do open Golf convertibles crawl the perimeters of our parks, scouts standing in the back, Zeiss binoculars ever on the *qui vive* for lob and volley? I fear not. Something... call it the way I have of leaning on the net-post, coughing... tells me it is not my quality of shot that has commended me, but simply our old friend Big Microchip, who watches our every commercial move, via credit card records. I can only think that some sporting purchase of mine, some piece of leading-edge kit designed to squeeze one more percentage point out of the seemingly unimprovable game of the truly gifted – a revolutionary new arch-support, perhaps, a quantum leap on the liniment front – has alerted the VWLTA to my potential.

Potential? Not, I think, for international stardom, remunerative endorsements, or, in my honoured sunset, a chain of Mediterranean coaching centres, but for something a mite more mundane. I note from their communication that, if I register, I will not only receive generous discounts on Hertz car rental, RAC membership, selected insurance policies, tennis holidays and much else besides; I will also automatically enter the Prize Draw for Sergio Tacchini tennis socks, Pro-Kennex tennis racquets, Penn tennis balls, Club Sportif tennis hols in Kenya, and, yes, a VW Golf. Which is probably due for relaunch as the VW Tennis any moment now.

Alan Coren, Diary, *The Times*, 30.3.89, page 16

★ ★ ★

One day the excellent trainer and gent Jeremy Tree approached Lester Piggott (Britain's greatest jockey), 'I've got to speak to my old school, Lester, all the boys at Eton, and tell them all I know about racing. What shall I say?' A pause and then the mumbled answer, 'Tell 'em you've got flu.'
Jeffrey Bernard, *Spectator*, 22.10.88

\* \* \*

Dr Bernard Richards, fellow of Brasenose, tells the story in the *Oxford Magazine* of the former principal of his college who regretfully turned down a superb athlete applying for admission.

'Even we,' he said, 'could not take a man who spells Jesus with a small g.'
Kenneth Rose, *Sunday Telegraph*, 10.2.91, page 9

\* \* \*

Samuel Johnson described fishing as a worm at one end and a fool at the other.

\* \* \*

An English merchant banker desperate to acquire tickets for the World Rugby Cup Finals in South Africa decided that he had to make the ultimate sacrifice. He put an advert in a newspaper offering 'Matrimony in exchange for two tickets to the World Rugby Cup Final'.

The first letter he opened said 'Offer accepted, please send photograph of tickets.'
*Financial Times*, 25.5.95

\* \* \*

It is a difference of opinion that makes horse-races.
Mark Twain

\* \* \*

'The accidents that befell these eight men happened during the recent celebrations to mark the fifty-second anniversary of the end of Japanese rule,' a medical spokesman told journalists in Taiwan. 'A mass tug-of-war contest was organized in the park with sixteen hundred contestants, eight hundred on either side. It seems that these eight men wrapped the rope around their left arms before the contest began, so they could get a better grip. But unfortunately the rope snapped seconds after the event started and, in the ensuing chaos, the men had their arms ripped out of their bodies. It was not a nice sight. Some onlookers vomited.

All the injuries were very similar, and there was some difficulty in ascertaining which arm belonged to which man, so yes, we may initially have sewed some of the wrong ones on. However, we were quick to remedy the errors once they were pointed out to us, and we are now fairly certain that we have reattached all the arms correctly. This sort of activity has to stop.

*Hospital Doctor*, 30.4.98, quoted by Dr Alan Cohen in *Private Eye*, July 1998

# The Ravenous Eye

*(Television)*

Television is chewing gum for the eyes.
Frank Lloyd Wright

\* \* \*

The public is not really concerned with atomic fallout, because so far it has not affected television reception.

\* \* \*

If TV had covered the crucifixion, the cameras would have packed it in just before the third day.
Oliver Pritchett

\* \* \*

There is no more cogent argument for the televising of Parliament than the sight of MPs of different persuasions, huddling together for warmth in the night, as they wait to be interviewed in Parliament Square. The drifting snow settles on them like bird lime on statues. The blast lifts the last of their hair. People point at them in the street. Elderly members I have never heard of in my life before are flung incontinently into cabs and ordered, on arrival, to discourse on leaks. Plump members of sedentary habits attempt to appear simultaneously in studios at opposite ends of London, ministers are grilled like chops first thing on Sunday morning, while an unshaven nation mocks their socks. It is all quite frightful and keeps me awake nights.
Nancy Banks-Smith, *Guardian*, 25.1.86

\* \* \*

Last week on *Clive James on Television*, a survey of the world's air waves, we saw clips from far-flung versions of our own nightly fare – *Japanese Candid Camera*, Spanish *Fawlty Towers* and so on. Funniest and most embarrassing was a glimpse of the rewards offered on a Nigerian quiz show: tonight's star prize was a paperback of *Jaws 2*. It reminded you of a window-display in a top Kampala department store during the reign of Idi Amin: the display consisted of a broken toaster and one gym-shoe.

Martin Amis, TV column, *Observer*, 3.10.82

★ ★ ★

Australian television has a reputation for being the most educational in the world, largely because it's so bad it makes you want to read a book.

Mark Wallington, *Daily Mail*, 25.8.88

★ ★ ★

Last week the management of this station wished our viewers a Happy New Year. Here is Mr Herbert Wilbur with an opposing view.

Cartoon in the *New Yorker*

★ ★ ★

'We are what you made us,' a member of the terrorist gang of Charles Manson who murdered actress Sharon Tate and others, explained. 'We were brought up watching *Gunsmoke*, *Have Gun Will Travel*, *FBI*, *Combat*. *Combat* was my favourite show. I never missed *Combat*.'

Conor Cruise O'Brien, *Observer*, 9.8.82

★ ★ ★

This medium is bound to deceive: even if you put the truth into it, it comes out a deception.

Malcolm Muggeridge, in *The New Priesthood* by Joan Bakewell

★ ★ ★

TV's power for good or evil is roughly equivalent to that of the hula-hoop.

Keith Waterhouse, *Punch*, 2.7.66

★ ★ ★

TV encourages people to buy luxuries who can't afford necessities.

★ ★ ★

Channel 4 has a peculiar way of sensing whether its programmes are in danger of offending taste and decency guidelines. Erect penises are a complete no-no in television land but of course during particularly saucy scenes a degree of tumescence is inevitable. How far can they go? Enter the 'angle of dangle' device. Producers refer to a map of Scotland and in particular to the Mull of Kintyre. If the offending implement raises its head above the angle of the peninsula then it's out. If it doesn't, it's in. And with Nick Broomfield's film on fetishism on its way, such distinctions are going to be important.

*Guardian*, 7.9.98

# When the Curtain Falls
### (Theatre and Playwrights)

Joan Littlewood once remarked that there are so few of us who actually like the theatre that we can't afford to quarrel.
William Gaskill interviewed by Sheridan Morley, *The Times*, 6.8.82

\* \* \*

We all know the chestnut about the old lady who saw *Hamlet* for the first time and came out complaining that it was full of quotations. But there is also an unintended point in the story: it was Shakespeare's unique ability to clothe a thought, original or familiar, profound or trivial, in words that have rooted themselves in the innermost consciousness of millions. If you have no idea what I am talking about and declare, 'It's Greek to me,' you are quoting Shakespeare; if you insist that your lost dog has vanished 'into thin air' you are quoting Shakespeare; if you narrowly avoid being run over and call the errant driver 'a blinking idiot', you are quoting Shakespeare.
Bernard Levin, *Listener*, 26.8.82

\* \* \*

If *Hamlet* had been written these days it would probably have been called *The Strange Affair at Elsinore*.
Sir James Barrie

\* \* \*

Changing theatre agents is like changing deckchairs on the *Titanic*.

\* \* \*

Every woman wants to play Hamlet just as every man wants to play Lady Bracknell.
W H Auden

\* \* \*

If we wish to know the force of human genius we should read Shakespeare. If we wish to see the insignificance of human learning we may study his commentators.
William Hazlitt

\* \* \*

He didn't believe the works of Shakespeare were written by Shakespeare but by someone else of the same name.
Mark Twain

\* \* \*

Audiences, like salad dressing, are never the same.
Robert Morley

\* \* \*

The attempt to reconcile the poetry which Shakespeare wrote with the prose of the extremely prosaic life he led is apt to addle the brains of those who undertake it.
Logan Pearsall Smith, quoted by Helen Gardner, *Spectator*, 26.3.83

\* \* \*

Tragedy is about incurable, comedy about curable, suffering.
Nietzsche, quoted in a review of *Kleist*, *Financial Times*, 7.1.84

\* \* \*

A Hungarian playwright, annoyed by decisions of director Laszlo Brothy to cut many of his lines, was finally provoked into protest. 'No play ever failed because of the lines that were cut out,' he said, 'only by the ones that were left in.'

Told by George Mikes at the Garrick, 4.8.86

\* \* \*

A woman on hearing Macbeth say, 'Tomorrow and tomorrow and tomorrow,' remarked to her companion, 'So that'll be Monday then.'

Sheridan Morley, *The Times*, 30.12.88

\* \* \*

George S Kaufman visited a play he had directed and found the star had changed bits of business and revised lines. He sent a note to the star's dressing room. 'I am standing in the back of the stalls. Wish you were here.'

\* \* \*

Eric Maschwitz, co-author of the musical *Good Night Vienna*, found himself waiting for a train on a wet night in Lewisham. At the local theatre he saw they were playing his musical and in the foyer he saw the manager waiting for the final curtain. Introducing himself, he asked how the show was doing. Said the manager: 'It's doing as well as *Good Night Lewisham* would do in Vienna.'

\* \* \*

Farce is always about the worst day in your life.

Jonathan Lynn (actor and director)

\* \* \*

Showing at London's Royal Court Theatre is *Death and the Maiden*, a thriller set in the aftermath of Chilean dictatorship. One night, by chance, Juliet Stevenson's character meets a man whom she thinks is the doctor who tortured her fifteen years ago. At Saturday's matinée, Stevenson suffered a cataclysmic nose bleed and the traditional call went out: 'Is there a doctor in the house?' The woman who answered this appeal was rewarded by a yell from the gods: 'Juliet, don't trust the doctor!'

\* \* \*

Terence Rattigan and I (John Osborne) had a desultory, forlorn correspondence for a while. His letters were written in the small hours, usually from Paris or Bermuda. They were cautious, courteous and generous. There was a great deal of regret for his past, confessions of professional dishonesty and avarice as well as advice about not deserting my country to live among tax-reprobates, how to withstand the sustained vilification of reviewers and, worst of all, the desertion of your public. Never having had the last, it was the least useful insight. 'Whatever you do, and I don't think you will,' he said, 'don't write what they expect you to write.' No one knew better that playwrights are especially condemned to the yawn and spite of fashion. Their work lays them open to something like social banishment while novelists and poets are more comfortably barricaded in their studies. If they are successful in their twenties and persist in working on into the decrepitude of their early fifties, only uncompensated redundancy faces them until they receive the country's gold watch when terminal illness and death qualify them for reassessment.

No one suffered more evidently from this assault course than Rattigan and Coward. Noël, with his justified arrogance, 'rose above it' in the discovery of his newly acclaimed genius in cabaret. Rattigan, introspective in a manner which the Master would have regarded as self-indulgent, was permanently wounded, exiling himself to Beverly Hills and

**Sir Terence Rattigan**

colonial golf clubs. The irony is that they were never really out of fashion at all. They simply allowed themselves to be convinced of it by a few hacks and hustlers.

John Osborne, *Spectator*, 3.8.85, page 7

★ ★ ★

After W H Auden had briefly and disastrously collaborated with Bertolt Brecht on a version of *The Duchess of Malfi*, he concluded that Brecht was the only person he had ever met who justified the existence of capital punishment.

Sean French, *The Times*, 28.12.96, page 18

★ ★ ★

Satire is something that closes Saturday night.

George S Kaufman

★ ★ ★

Peter Brook the producer recalled that when he worked in Covent Garden, in the late 1940s, the electricians would sometimes miss the lighting cues because they were so entranced by the music. 'I suddenly realized,' he said, 'how useful it is not to like what you are doing.'

Michael Billington, *Guardian*, 12.5.89

★ ★ ★

The new trustees of the National Heritage Memorial Fund have wide discretion. Their latest report includes a grant of £50,000 to the British Library for the purchase of Sir Terence Rattigan's papers. It contains this letter of 1954 from his fellow playwright Noël Coward:

My dear Terry – Both the plays are superbly written,

241

beautifully constructed and rich with a deep understanding of human nature. I was profoundly impressed. They are also impeccably directed and most gloriously acted. What more can I say, except to send you my love and congratulations?

Noël

PS   Write a bad play soon, there's a dear boy, so that I can write you a tiny carping letter. I'm sick of all this slush.
Kenneth Rose, *Sunday Telegraph*, 2.12.90

★ ★ ★

Commenting on Lionel Bart's musical *Blitz!*, about the Battle of Britain, Noël Coward said, 'It was twice as loud and twice as long as the real thing.'

★ ★ ★

Harold Pinter's latest play was very short with critics uncertain about whether it was eight or nine minutes long. 'It was actually six minutes long,' said one. 'But it seemed like eight.'
August 1991

★ ★ ★

The death of Sheridan (1750–1816) prompted a long obituary in *The Times*, one compounded of eulogy, censure and moralising.

MR SHERIDAN

It is with deep regret we announce to our readers the death of the Right Honourable Richard Brinsley Sheridan, who, after a severe and protracted illness, expired yesterday at noon.

The astonishing talent for observation, and knowledge of

character, displayed by Mr Sheridan in his dramatic writings, will surprise us more when we recollect that he composed *The Rivals* whilst yet a boy; and that his *School for Scandal* was written at four and twenty. Those who are best acquainted with the history of the stage for an hundred years preceding their appearance, can best appreciate the obligations of the public to an author whose dialogue has the spirit of reality without its coarseness, whose sentiment is animated, his wit refined...

If we pursue Mr Sheridan into political life, we shall have equal cause to admire the vigour and versatility of his genius. The field on every side of him was occupied by the ablest men who had appeared in Parliament for more than half a century. Burke...Pitt and Fox...these were formidable checks to the rise of an adventurer not recommended by character nor connexion, beset by a thousand mischievous bits – crusted over with indolence and depressed by fortune...

He distinguished himself amongst them by wielding with success the various weapons for which they were respectively celebrated. In flow of diction he yielded not even to Mr Pitt – in force and acuteness he might justly be compared with the great Opposition Leader; while in splendour of imagination he equalled Burke, and in its use and management far excelled him...

It has been made a reproach by some persons, in lamenting Mr Sheridan's cruel destiny, that 'his friends' had not done more for him. We freely and conscientiously declare it as our opinion, that had Mr Sheridan enjoyed ten receiverships of Cornwall instead of one, he would not have died in affluence. He never would have attained to comfort or independence in his fortune...a man who is inveterately thoughtless of consequences, and callous to reproof – who knows not when he squanders money, because he feels not those obligations which constitute or direct its uses – such a man it is impossible to rescue from destruction...But what friends are blamed for neglecting Mr Sheridan? What friendships did he ever form? The fact is, that a life of conviviality and intemperance seldom favours the cultivation of those better tastes and affections which are necessary to the existence of intimate friendship...

We have now performed an honest duty, and in many particulars an humbling and most distressing one we have found it. Never were such gifts as those which Providence showered upon Mr Sheridan so abused – never were talents so miserably perverted...

On This Day, *The Times*, 8.7.88

\* \* \*

Theo Cowan's apartment always looked as if the proverbial bomb had hit it. He told a wonderful story about an occasion when Peter Sellers was feeling down and rang him to ask him to spend the evening with him. Cowan was none too keen on doing this and it must have been apparent in his voice as Sellers immediately said that if it was too much bother he would come round to his home instead. This threw Cowan into a blind panic. No doubt many of his star clients assumed that he lived in the same kind of penthouse splendour as they did. How could he disguise the chaos?

In typically quick-witted fashion he found the solution. He shot into the garage and dragged in a couple of step-ladders and a plank. He erected them in the sitting-room and put some paint brushes and old pots of paint on top. He took some white sheets and completely covered everything in the room. In came Sellers who perched on the dustsheet-covered sofa (on which were now safely hidden old pipes, tobacco tins, seed packets, etc) and apologized for intruding when he was in the midst of redecorating.

Alan Capper, obituary of Theo Cowan (entertainment-industry publicist), *Independent*, 18.9.91

# Wars are for Winning

*(War and the Military)*

There is no greater fatuity than a political judgement dressed in a military uniform.

Lloyd-George

★ ★ ★

Military intelligence is a contradiction in terms.

Groucho Marx

★ ★ ★

Frederick the Great once said that if he wished to punish a conquered province very severely he would condemn it to being governed by men of letters – a far worse fate, in his view, than being put to the sword.

Peregrine Worsthorne, *Sunday Telegraph*, 1.8.82

★ ★ ★

A Falkland Island is a small piece of land entirely surrounded by advice.

Penelope Gilliat, 'Authors Take Sides on The Falklands', *Sunday Telegraph*

★ ★ ★

It is not for the sheep to pass resolutions in favour of vegetarianism if the wolf holds a different opinion.

Dean Inge, talking about peace movements between the wars

★ ★ ★

After the battle the king may dispose of my head as he will, but during the battle he will kindly allow me to make use of it.
General Seydlitz at the Battle of Lorndorf

* * *

Artemus Ward, President Lincoln's favourite, in a patriotic speech during the American Civil War said, 'I have already given three cousins to the war, and I stand prepared to sacrifice my wife's brother rather than that the rebellion be not crushed.'
Robert Conquest, *Daily Telegraph*, 23.2.85

* * *

No other army (than the English) has ever gone into war proclaiming its own incompetence and reluctance to fight, and no army has fought better.
A J P Taylor, quoted in Godfrey Smith's *The English Companion*, page 20

* * *

General Eric Dorman Smith, nicknamed 'Chink', was deputy chief of staff to General Auchinleck. He was unjustly blamed for the defeat at Gazala in 1942. The main reproach against him was that he was too intellectual. He never lived down the shame of scoring a thousand points out of a thousand at staff college.
Richard Pryne, *Sunday Telegraph*, 24.8.86

* * *

In war, truth is so precious it must always be accompanied by a bodyguard of lies.
Winston Churchill in *Closing the Ring*, volume V of his memoirs

* * *

In the row about whether German military men should be involved with the fiftieth anniversary of D-Day on 6 June 1994, Godfrey Smith in the *Sunday Times* recalled that an MP questioned as improper fraternization Montgomery's decision after the Allied victory in North Africa – he was a vegetarian and ascetic – to invite the captured German general to lunch in his tent. Churchill jumped to his feet. 'Poor von Thoma,' he said feelingly, 'I, too, have had lunch with Montgomery.'
*Sunday Times*, 27.3.94

\* \* \*

Loopy (alias Lieutenant Colonel Sir George Kennard, Bart) is elegant, witty and courageous. His Grace is also insufferable – patronizing to his inferiors and disloyal to his superiors. He is an élitist, a hedonist, a dilettante, an amateur who refuses to do anything he considers unsuitable for a gentleman – such as mastering, as opposed to dabbling in, a profession, or – heaven forbid – keeping accounts.

I remember Loopy. When he was commanding 4th Hussars at Hohne in BAOR, in 1955, I was a junior officer in an adjoining gunner regiment. Many stories were current about him. One was that before an exercise he had spoken to the officers as follows: 'Gentlemen, on the forthcoming exercise, the corps commander has directed that 1 British Corps will live hard; I have been giving this thought, and I think we must make a gesture. We will go out without tablecloths or mineral water.'

I hope the old reprobate can live out his days in contentment and reasonable comfort in Devon. One of his good qualities is the ability to give and inspire affection. It would be sad to see the end of the style and elegance which men like Loopy bring to English life. But such men should never be given responsibility. In war, they lead their men to disaster. In peace, they lead their businesses to bankruptcy. If you wish to see why this nation has declined, read this infuriating, charming, obscene and brilliant book.
Sidney Vines, reviewing *Loopy* by George Kennard, *Spectator*, 19.1.91

\* \* \*

A captured German diary in Normandy had this entry:

June 18, 1941 – Washday
June 19, 1941 – Washday
June 20, 1941 – War with Russia
June 21, 1941 – Washday

★ ★ ★

Kill one man and you are a murderer, kill millions and you are a conqueror. Kill everybody and you are God.

Jean Rostand, *Dictionary of War Quotations*, edited by Justin Wintle

★ ★ ★

I have never understood this liking for war. It panders to instincts already catered for within the scope of any respectable domestic establishment.

Alan Bennett, ibid.

★ ★ ★

In America's attitude to the prospect of war [in the Gulf], there is something deeper at work. Perhaps the United States is no longer fitted for the part of global power, because it now regards death as an unacceptable decline in an American's standard of living.

Frank Johnson, *Sunday Telegraph*, 4.11.90

★ ★ ★

What shocked me on entering battle was the speed with which surrounding might seemed to thin out, and one found oneself no longer part of a mighty host, but confronting marked unpleasantness in a muddy field with only a few chums. That is where, according to the book, the confidence of the soldier in his weapons comes in – though I never found it so.

Unexpectedly, in extremely nasty situations one came to depend heavily on the soldier, probably a busted sergeant, who had a fairly awful peacetime record for absence, reckless driving, drunkenness, fornication and insolence to seniors. In the last ditch, he was a rock; possibly because he wanted to prove you had done the right thing by sticking to him. I devoutly hope they have some of those in the desert.

W F Deedes, *Daily Telegraph*, 14.1.91, page 16

# The Imperious Sex

*(Women)*

Djuna Barnes was a writer and friend of James Joyce and T S Eliot in Paris of the 1920s. A boastful male once spoke to her of the beauties of the penis, saying it could even write a sentence on the snow; could a woman's organ do that? A woman, said Djuna Barnes, could at least provide a period.

Book review by Anthony Burgess, *Observer*, 21.8.83

\* \* \*

A man with two women loses his soul;
A man with two homes loses his mind.

Alfred de Musset, quoted by David Castell, *Sunday Telegraph*, 11.11.84, page 18

\* \* \*

A man's mother is his misfortune; his wife is his fault.

Walter Bagehot

\* \* \*

Sir – I was delighted to read in the Odd Man Out column by Martyn Harris that he felt women spent too much time doing unnecessary housework. People often ask me how I manage to find the time for all the things that I do. I tell them that I never dust, don't clean the windows until the sun can no longer penetrate the dirt and wash the kitchen floor only when the pattern of the tiles is no longer discernible.

As a result I have three healthy, happy children with whom

I often have time to play, I work as a midwife most weekends and interpret for deaf children and adults during the week. I have had my first novel published and a short story read on the radio.

I even have time to write to the papers.

Candy Denman, Waltham Cross, Herts

Letter to *Daily Telegraph*, 22.4.88

\* \* \*

It's very easy for women to get dressed up for an evening, you know. They can wear old curtains and things.

Philip Hope-Wallace

\* \* \*

I fear nothing so much as a man who is witty all day long.

Madame de Sévingé

\* \* \*

The Englishwoman is so refined she has no bosom and no behind.

Stevie Smith, 'This Englishwoman'

\* \* \*

A few days ago you were a divine. Now you are a woman.

Baudelaire to Madame Sabatier, to whom he sent poems anonymously for five years; when she responded to his courtship he beat a retreat

\* \* \*

Never marry a man who hates his mother or he'll end up hating you.

Jill Bennett, quoted by Lynda Lee-Potter, *Daily Mail*, 15.9.82

\* \* \*

'A baby girl – how lovely,' people said . . . I extended a tentative would-be velvety finger and found it seized in an iron fist. Pebble-dark eyes, as hard too in their stare, had scrutinised me under a surprising amount of dark hair. It was more like meeting Napoleon.

Sir Michael Levey (director of the National Gallery)

★ ★ ★

Women never dine alone. When they dine alone they don't dine.

Henry James

★ ★ ★

When the Garrick Club votes on Tuesday week whether or not to admit women, I'm told just a few words written by John Osborne could sway one or two members previously intent on voting women in.

'Should this barmy ballot be carried,' John wrote in the *Spectator* last week, 'the pleasures of masculine courtliness and hospitality will be gone . . . that mysterious mixture of discretion, reticence and flamboyance will be banished forever.' It reminds me of Kipling saying the loveliest sound in the world was 'deep-voiced men laughing together over dinner'.

Nowadays remarks like that are deemed sexist, chauvinist, politically incorrect and, for all I know, actionable. You have to be a Kipling or Osborne to get away with them: wordsmiths people love or hate but never forget.

Godfrey Smith, *Sunday Times*, 28.6.92

★ ★ ★

Were it not for gold and women, there would be no damnation.

Cyril Tourneur (Elizabethan playwright)

★ ★ ★

If you give women a chance, we can perform. After all, Ginger Rogers did everything Fred Astaire did. She just did it backwards in high heels.

Mrs Ann Richards, in keynote address at US Democratic Convention to select Dukakis in Atlanta on 19 July 1988, *Daily Telegraph*, 20.7.88, page 7

* * *

Only *The Media Show* (Channel 4), surely, could introduce a feminist note into a discussion of TV's coverage of natural history. One of two women journalists being interviewed on Sunday's programme objected to the emphasis which wildlife programmes place on the male aggression of hunting, and the extent to which the animal world is seen as being concerned with reproduction. I've frequently tutted over these aspects of nature myself, but I've always thought that criticisms should be directed towards the Almighty, for arranging matters so blatantly, rather than at Sir David Attenborough, who only observes His handiwork.

Richard Last, *Daily Telegraph*, 2.10.90

* * *

Why, often enough, are the women better-looking, better-dressed and more likely to behave in a feminine manner in places that are old-fashioned, and even politically confused, such as Italy was and, according to Signor Severgnini, still is?

Burke rather foresaw some of this two hundred years ago. He remarked that, in an age of women's rights – which he foresaw in the United States, the great country of formal rights – the women would become ugly and you would be sued in the courts if you presented them with a bunch of flowers (something like this has happened in New York). Of progressive left-wing movements in general, a character in one of Arthur Koestler's novels remarks, in the context of Communist internationalists: 'There must be something wrong with a movement whose women are so ugly.'

Professor Norman Stone, *Evening Standard*, 15.8.91

* * *

I have never seen two identically dressed women in the streets of London. Trivial at first glance, this impression is an accurate portrayal of the serious role of private pleasure in the life of the West, of the boundless stamina and astronomical variety of a commercial civilization.

Andrei Navrozov (a Russian journalist living in Britain), *Guardian*, 13.8.91

* * *

The tragedy was she was just getting her hair right.

Hairdresser on hearing of Princess Diana's death, 10.9.97

* * *

They've just sunk the *Titanic* – again. This time, it was a bunch of lawyers at the American Bar Association's annual beano in Toronto. A day has just been used up in a fictional lawsuit brought by a 'survivor' of the 1912 tragedy against White Star Line, which owned and operated the ship, and Harland and Wolff, the Belfast shipyard that built her. Attorney Chilton Davis Varner of Atlanta, representing the shipyard, painted White Star as the villain, given that it overruled Harland and Wolff's advice to provide enough lifeboats for all the passengers. The absence of binoculars for the lookouts didn't help either.

But the jury of top lawyers said the shipbuilder was liable and awarded £900,000 in damages. The owners, however, might not have escaped entirely. The 'survivor' announced that her husband had perished only because of the 'women and children first' instruction to passengers. So she would pursue White Star Line for sex discrimination.

Observer, *Financial Times*, 5.8.98

# Fortunes are for Others

*(Work, Business and Advertising)*

An advertising man was asked for a campaign to sell white tuna fish where the public was conditioned to eating pink tuna. He got a large sum and a year later still hadn't come up with a plan. Finally pressed by the clients he took out a crumpled piece of paper and said, 'Paste that on every can.' It was a great success. The words on the paper read: 'This tuna is guaranteed not to turn pink in the can.'

Story told by Jim Deacon, *St Louis Post Dispatch*, May 1977

\* \* \*

Trying to promote their washing powder Lux in Africa, the manufacturers Lever Bros ran a special offer: 'Free beads with every pack.' A European salesman, with his African driver, set off to distribute the product to African villages. But after visiting three villages, he'd sold no stock at all. At this point the African driver said he would do the next village. He drove off with the supplies – and came back having got rid of the lot.

'How did you do it?' asked the Lever Bros man.

'Easy, bwana. I sold the beads and gave away the soap.'

Michael Watts, *Sunday Express*, 12.12.82

\* \* \*

I love work – I can sit and watch it all day long.

Jerome K Jerome

\* \* \*

Buy land, my son, they are not making any more.

Mark Twain, quoted by Clement Freud, *The Times*, 9.5.88

\* \* \*

My great childhood hero was the man reputed to have gone to the Swan Vesta match company and entered into a deal whereby he would receive fifty per cent of the savings achieved by adopting his proposal. When the agreement was finally drawn up and the lawyers had assembled managerial, technical, operational and union representatives to gauge the merits of his plan of action the man said: 'If you put sandpaper on one side of the box instead of on both sides, you'd save half the sandpaper.' He is now very rich, living in Bognor Regis.

I mention him because I met the chairman and managing director of the Hot Foot Corporation of Western Australia. He is here on holiday but not averse to talking business. Hot Foot has patented and produces a roof paint that is tacky and malodorous, causing pigeons that land thereon to depart instantaneously and relieve themselves on the roof of some other building whose owner has not had the foresight to utilize Hot Foot's product. We were standing in Trafalgar Square, looking up at the Column. I think I saw Nelson nod.

Clement Freud, *The Times*, 30.5.88

\* \* \*

Outside the New York Stock Exchange office of leading stockbroker John Phelan, framed in mahogany, is the following quotation from Machiavelli's *The Prince*: 'There is nothing more difficult to take in hand, more perilous to conduct, or more uncertain in its success, than to take the lead in the introduction of a new order of things.'

Carl Leonard, City Diary, *The Times*, 26.1.88

\* \* \*

An old Spanish joke has someone calling at a ministry and asking to see a junior bureaucrat. 'He's not here,' the visitor is told, to which he replies, 'Isn't he working this morning?' 'No, no,' it is explained to him, 'It's the afternoons that he doesn't work. In the morning he's not in.'

*Time*, 5.1.83, page 4

\* \* \*

A bank manager rang one of his minions seeking data on a client.

'Too busy,' came the brusque reply.

The manager repeated the request, but in vain. 'Do you know who you're talking to?' he asked testily. 'I am the manager.'

There was a pause at the other end of the line and then came an anxious: 'Do you know who you are talking to?'

'No,' said the manager.

The minion's voice sounded warmer.

'That's a relief – Goodbye.'

*Financial Times*, 2.9.87

\* \* \*

Overheard at a company reception in a Birmingham hotel: 'He could sell Father's Day cards to unmarried mothers.'

Diary, *Daily Telegraph*, 25.8.83

\* \* \*

Work is something that when we have it we wish we did not; when we do not have it we wish we did; and the object of most of it is to be able to afford not to do any someday.

Quote from a local paper in the US, in the City Diary of *The Times*, 8.2.90

\* \* \*

George wrote to me from Yorkshire about his forty-seven-year-old son, Joe, who after a long jobless period turned to studying. The other day Joe had his six-monthly interview at the Job Centre under the Restart programme.

'We notice you are still unemployed after six months.'

'Eleven years six months, to be exact.'

'Where are you willing to work?'

'Anywhere.'

'You're not allowed to say "anywhere". What was your previous job?'

'Van driver.'

'What kind of work are you looking for and what have you been doing to get work of this kind?'

'University lecturer and I read the appointments pages.'

'Have you any qualifications?'

'Diploma in Art and Design; BA (Hons) Humanities; MA Local History; Certificate in Business Information and Technology Skills; Certificate in Teaching English to Speakers of Other Languages. And I'm doing a PhD part time.'

'What have you been doing to find work?'

Joe produces details of certificates and three years of job applications. After reading these, the interviewer comments that there are not many lecturing jobs. 'You must be prepared to work in other fields. What jobs are you prepared to apply for?'

'Administrative and clerical.'

'Have you any administrative and clerical experience?'

'No.'

'What work are you experienced in?'

'Eleven years ago I was a van driver.'

'We'll put your first choice as van driver and your second choice as clerical/administrative. Do you agree with this?'

'Yes.'

'Thank you. Bye-bye.'

'Bye-bye. See you in six months.'

What really impresses me about this story is George's comment that it gave the two of them a good laugh.

Ruth Dudley Edwards, *Guardian*, 10.4.95

★ ★ ★

A hot-air balloonist realizes he is lost. He spots a man down below, reduces height and shouts: 'Excuse me, can you tell me where I am?'

The man below says: 'Yes, you're in a basket below a hot air balloon, hovering thirty feet above this field.'

'You must work in information technology,' says the balloonist.

'I do,' replies the man. 'How did you know?'

'Well,' says the balloonist, 'everything you have told me is technically correct, but it's no use to anyone.'

The man below says, 'You must be a corporate manager.'

'I am,' replies the balloonist, 'but how did you know?'

'Well,' says the man, 'you don't know where you are, or where you're going, but you expect me to help. You're in the same position you were before we met, but now it's my fault.'

Observer, *Financial Times*, 1.9.98

# You've Heard it Before
### (Wits)

### DOROTHY PARKER

At a party where the guests were playing a game called 'ducking for apples', Dorothy Parker commented: 'There but for a typographical error, is the story of my life.'

* * *

It is not a book to be tossed aside lightly. It should be thrown across a room with great force.

* * *

Why is it that no one ever sent me yet one perfect limousine,
   do you suppose?
Ah no, it's always just my luck to get one perfect rose.

* * *

> Razors pain you;
> Rivers are damp;
> Acids stain you;
> And drugs give cramp.
> Guns are unlawful;
> Nooses give;
> Gas smells awful –
> You might as well live.

'Résumé', (1937)

* * *

When Dorothy Parker was asked if she knew the painter Augustus John, she replied: 'Well enough to call him Augustus Jack.'

## GEORGE BERNARD SHAW

A lifetime of happiness! No man alive could bear it; it would be hell on earth.

★ ★ ★

Never strike a child in anger – and then strike to kill.

★ ★ ★

Shaw said of Brahms's German Requiem, 'It has made so many of us wish we were dead.'

## W C FIELDS

On the whole, I'd rather be in Philadelphia.
Last words.

★ ★ ★

I never drink water. Fish fuck in it.

★ ★ ★

The first thing to do when you get up in the morning is smile. Get it over with.

★ ★ ★

Anyone who hates children and animals can't be all bad.

★ ★ ★

When W C Fields was caught scanning a Bible, he explained that he was 'looking for loopholes'.

★ ★ ★

W C Fields had quarrelled with an assistant after a performance. 'You're fired,' growled Fields. 'Then I'll get a job at RKO,' retorted the assistant. 'They're all Jews at RKO,' said Fields. 'No, they're not Jews,' said the assistant, 'they are Roman Catholics.' 'The worst kind of Jews,' came back Fields.
*Faber Book of Anecdotes*, 1985


## GROUCHO MARX

I never forget a face, but in your case I'll make an exception.

★ ★ ★

Groucho Marx taking the pulse of an unconscious man says, 'Either he's dead or my watch has stopped.'

★ ★ ★

In *A Night at the Opera*, Groucho, as impresario Otis B Driftwood, asks the illiterate Chico to sign a contract.

| | |
|---|---|
| Chico: | You read it. |
| Groucho: | All right. I'll read it to you. Can you hear? |
| Chico: | I haven't heard anything yet, did you say anything? |
| Groucho: | Well, I haven't said anything worth hearing. |

| Chico: | Well, that's why I didn't hear anything. |
| Groucho: | Well, that's why I didn't say anything. |

\* \* \*

When Groucho Marx was refused entry to an exclusive Long Island swimming club that didn't admit Jews, he said, 'What about my son? He's only half-Jewish. Would it be all right if he went in up to his knees?'

*My Life with Groucho* by Arthur Marx (Robson Books, 1988)

\* \* \*

Interviewing a tree surgeon on his TV quiz programme *You Bet Your Life*, Groucho asked, 'Tell me, doctor, did you ever fall out of a patient?'

\* \* \*

Asked on his eighty-second birthday how he would like to be remembered, Groucho said, 'Alive. If not that way, then dead.'

## NOËL COWARD

Seeing Randolph Churchill leave a cocktail party after a row, Noël Coward said, 'There goes poor Randolph, completely unspoilt by failure.'

\* \* \*

Only station-masters wear roses in their buttonholes

\* \* \*

On seeing Anna Neagle as Queen Victoria in *The Glorious*

*Years*, Coward said: 'That's the first time I realized Albert had married beneath his station.'

* * *

Noël Coward was watching the parade that followed on the Queen's coronation. The crowds were particularly taken with the massive and beaming Queen of Tonga, who waved good-naturedly to all as she rode by in the rain. Beside her in the carriage was a very small man in a top hat. 'Who's that next to the Queen of Tonga?' asked someone. 'Her lunch,' was Coward's crisp reply.

* * *

On a Nazi blacklist discovered in 1945, Noël Coward's name was prominent among the English political and literary figures to be liquidated in the event of a German victory. Rebecca West, who had been on the same list, sent him a telegram which read: 'My dear – the people we should have been seen dead with!'

## SAMUEL GOLDWYN

That atom bomb . . . it's dynamite.

* * *

An oral contract isn't worth the paper it's written on.

* * *

Goldwyn was at open air concert in Chicago given by the violinist Jascha Heifetz. The auditorium was packed with sixty thousand spectators wildly enthusiastic about Heifetz's performance. So impressed was Goldwyn with the size of the audience and their enthusiasm that he decided to make a big film starring Heifetz. It was a very expensive flop. Said Goldwyn afterwards: 'Every one of those sixty thousand people came to see the picture – but nobody else.'

★ ★ ★

Let's have some new clichés.

★ ★ ★

I'll give you a definite maybe.

★ ★ ★

Anyone who goes to a psychiatrist needs his head examined.

★ ★ ★

Messages are for Western Union.

## VOLTAIRE

If God did not exist, it would be necessary to invent him.

★ ★ ★

It is one of the superstitions of the human mind to have imagined that virginity could be a virtue.

★ ★ ★

The way to be a bore...is to say everything.

★ ★ ★

In this country [England], it pays to shoot an admiral from time to time to encourage the others.

★ ★ ★

The superfluous – a very necessary thing.

★ ★ ★

I disapprove of what you say, but I will defend to the death your right to say it.


## OSCAR WILDE

One must have a heart of stone to read the death of Little Nell without laughing.
On Dickens's *The Old Curiosity Shop*

★ ★ ★

All women become like their mothers. That is their tragedy. No man does. That's his.

★ ★ ★

On coming out of prison, Oscar Wilde said admiringly to Mrs Leverson who had come to meet him, 'My dear, you're the only woman in the world who'd have known the right hat to wear on an occasion like this.'

★ ★ ★

Oscar Wilde once told a solicitous hostess that he had spent the morning adding a comma and had whiled away the afternoon removing it.
Edna O'Brien, *Observer*, 22.8.82

★ ★ ★

Oscar Wilde said of the American writer, Frank Harris: 'He is invited to all the great houses of England – once.'

★ ★ ★

After all, what is fashion? It is usually a form of ugliness so intolerable that we have to alter it every six months.

★ ★ ★

Oscar Wilde on his deathbed is reported to have said: 'This wallpaper is killing me. One of us will have to go.

# Index of Sources